C000184483

How to be a PA

A practical guide to becoming a super-efficient Personal Assistant

Everything you need to succeed as a PA. Full of practical tips for Personal Assistants, Executive Assistants, Office Managers, and Co-ordinators of Business Travel.

Maria Fuller

How to be a PA

Copyright © Maria Fuller 2016

All rights reserved. No part of this book may be reproduced or transmitted in any form or by any means without written permission from the author or publisher. Enquiries concerning reproduction, or for use as training material, should be sent to the author at **info@howtobeapa.co.uk**

The right of Maria Fuller to be identified as the author of this work has been asserted by her in accordance with the Copyright, Designs and Patents Act 1988.

ISBN 978-0-9933837-0-0

Published by Maria Fuller

What's in a name?

There are numerous job titles associated with the PA role, but for ease of consistency throughout this book, I am going to use the job title '**PA**'.

Chapter 3 explores the different role specialisms in further detail, and the exact job titles associated with them. It's also worth remembering that you should use both PA and EA in internet searches when researching educational or employment opportunities, or for further general research into the role.

It's also common place to use a multitude of terms when referring to our manager e.g. boss, line manager, director, team leader, supervisor, leader, head, minister, chief – again for ease of consistency I will use the term '**business executive**'.

Icons explained

Throughout How to be a PA you will see 3 different types of icons: 'Top Tips', 'Add to Bible' and 'For Action'. Use these as visual aids to find key insights and invaluable tips. Icons are explained in more detail below:

Top tips are golden nuggets of advice for PAs. Use them to increase your efficiency, improve processes and get ahead in the office.

Add to bible...

Every PA needs a **bible**. This is a document where you keep all your essential information together in one place. I use a word file for this, and add relevant information as and when appropriate e.g. travel preferences, how to book meeting rooms, conference bridge numbers, who to contact across different office locations, preferred hotels, favourite restaurants etc. It's a big reference file, which I use daily. 'Add to bible' icons flag up key points to add to your own PA bible.

Act now buttons are tasks for you to complete, as we progress through the different chapters. These are specific PA related exercises, to help you to become a super-efficient PA.

CONTENTS

1

Insider Knowledge

What's in this chapter?

Wouldn't it be great if executives extolled the virtues of their own personal assistant in a more public way? Gave credit where credits due, and recognised the professional capabilities required, in this truly remarkable role. In this chapter, 5 business leaders get an opportunity to do exactly that.

* Introduction
* Insights from business leaders

Introduction

The role of the personal assistant has evolved considerably, over the last decade. The support provided by a personal assistant, to a business executive, is far removed from the outdated perception of the traditional 'manager and secretary relationship'. Personal assistants have become micro managers, and are adept at problem solving, multi-tasking and providing reasoned observations, and insights, into the business. They provide the 'eyes and ears' for their executive, and are a constant and respected resource for senior business professionals.

PAs are also the unsung heroes in the office environment, and contribute substantially to the success of their manager. Members of the Board, high net worth individuals, entrepreneurs, and government ministers, all rely upon their personal assistants to support them with their day to day business life. To relieve them of the daily administration, travel management, diary management, and expense reporting. Plus ad hoc projects, event support, client entertainment, public relations and co-ordination of press interviews. This valuable human resource, assists the business executive to become more time efficient, work smarter, eliminates inefficiencies in the working day, and contributes to the success of the executive, and ultimately, the company, or organisation, for whom they work for.

As the PA role has matured, into a more dependable and justified resource for today's business executive, what is it that especially gets a PA noticed? How do you stand out as a PA and surpass your manager's expectations? What makes a truly exceptional PA? Unfortunately, due to confidentiality and company restrictions, we do not hear enough about exceptional PAs and what they did in order to stand out from the crowd. So I took the question out to a few of my personal contacts, and given the opportunity to share, they were very forthcoming. Here's what they said about their own PA experiences. A truly inspirational example for all PAs.

Insights from business leaders

Several prominent company executives were approached directly, to share with 'How to be a PA', examples of PA support which they had received, appreciated, and benefitted from in their careers. I am grateful to all contributors, and believe that the observations which follow provide a very useful insight into the PA/business executive relationship. Moreover, it demonstrates why the role of a personal assistant is so important, and beneficial to leaders, in today's business world.

Alastair Campbell, Director of Communications and Strategy for Prime Minister Tony Blair, 1997-2003
London, UK

"When we arrived in Downing Street in May 1997, we inherited a lot of the staff from John Major's Downing Street. My PA was Alison Blackshaw, whose first words to me were 'I really liked John Major.' We didn't gel well at first, partly because I was so used to doing everything for myself, but over time she became absolutely indispensable to me. She got to know my mind, knew when to put through calls and when not to, managed my diary without involving me with all the decisions that entailed, and most importantly, became an important part of the broader team. She was one of the few people in the building who could read the handwriting of Tony Blair, Jonathan Powell and me, so she was often expected to type up our scribbled notes into draft speeches.

I remember on one occasion, when we were on the way to the US for an important speech, she had typed up the latest draft. Tony was asking for it, I was at the back of the plane briefing the press and she was standing with the Prime Minister, as he read the draft. She said to him that she didn't normally give her opinion on these matters, but she was the only person apart from the rest of us, who had read every draft and she felt the first draft of several days ago was clearer. He asked to see it, read it, agreed and asked her to reinstate the speech opening we had earlier deleted.

What I liked about this, when she told me later, is that if the Prime Minister had not agreed, he would not have minded her raising her view. What I liked most of all, was that she felt sufficiently part of the team to know if she had a view, and felt strongly, she was entitled to raise it".

Liam Brown, Founder and Chairman, Elevate Services Inc.
Los Angeles, California, USA

"I cannot overemphasize the value of having someone around me that I completely trust, who does what they say they are going to do, is a great communicator, tells me what they really think (even if I don't want to hear it), who looks ahead for problems, and plans accordingly, and then when something unexpected and awful actually happens, remains cool, calm and decisive, to solve the problem. Tom Webster was all of those things for me.

Once, while we were hiring a new CFO, while everyone on the Executive Team and Board were pushing me to hire a particular candidate because she was an excellent technical and experience fit, Tom was the only person that told me that her personality would clash with our company culture, and not to hire her. Of course, I listened to everyone else, hired her and six months later he had the opportunity to tell me that he told me so, but of course didn't.

Another time, I had temporarily moved my whole family from Los Angeles to London for six months to help launch an industry leading initiative with a law firm client. I was on vacation in Mauritius when I received a call from Tom really early in the morning LA time. There had been a super storm, and trees had been blown over all over LA. He had driven out to check on my house and lo and behold a tree had been blown over and crashed onto the roof of our house, which was flooding with water. By the time he called me, he had already taken care of finding someone to tarp the roof and remove the tree.

How can I ever adequately express my gratitude to him for not only supporting my work, but supporting me and my family, when we needed help?"

11

Dr John H Newton,
Headmaster, Taunton School, Somerset, UK

"I have been blessed with one of the best read, most literate and most insightful PAs over the past 8 and a half years. When I arrived as Headmaster of this wonderful, but complex, school, I had no idea then just how impossible the job would be without Carol Cotton's assistance. I soon found out.

Carol could cope in any company, from the nervous 12 year olds waiting for scholarship interviews, to Lords and Ladies of the realm, who were my guests for various events. She did not flinch when General Sir Mike Jackson demanded whisky not coffee at 4 in the afternoon, and ensured Germaine Greer's bottle of Merlot was in the right place at the right time. She managed to keep her cool when the place was swarming with police on the visit of Lord and Lady Bannside, (the late Iain Paisley and his wife). Her capacity to make joyful conversation, to take an interest in the professional lives of such eminent people, made hospitality not only less of a chore, but a joy.

A boarding school is a village. It has a life and soul. One cannot be an intimate part of such a place and ignore the academic imperative, the concerts, the lecture series, the musicals, the plays, the debates, the chapel events, the sports programme.

Carol supported all of these, and therefore understood the inner dynamic of the place – its educational essence. Therefore she could do what all good PAs can do. She could read minds. She knew the significance of that anguished request for a meeting with the Director of Drama, or the Master in charge of Cricket. She knew who could wait and who should be ushered in. She set priorities just right so that the intricate workings of the place were not compromised, and the seemingly effortless success of the many events we put on had the right impact on pupils, staff, parents and the public at large.

School life is a calling. I expect that from my staff. Thankfully, I discovered that virtue in my PA".

Adam Gould, former Director of Commercial Services
Teleperformance, UK

"My PA, Maria Fuller, managed a hugely successful and highly unique company event, involving our Global Chairman and Global CEO. The event included VIP attendance, global travel co-ordination, an offsite and all-day meeting, with private dining and overnight accommodation, at the Hotel du Vin, Bristol. This was followed by a further day's itinerary with a site tour of our Bristol HQ, and our Bristol Moon Street operational site.

The event was not without its challenges! The Global Chairman and Founder of our organisation requested the event took place on May 27th- 28th, this was a UK public Holiday weekend! Whilst Maria did advise the Chairman's office, in Miami, that this was actually a UK Holiday, the Company Chairman had limited availability, so it was not possible to postpone the meeting, or his visit to the UK. We were advised to press ahead with the event co-ordination, and schedule across the Bank Holiday weekend.

As I'm sure you're aware, scheduling an event, on a Bank Holiday weekend, has many ramifications. Businesses are closed, external suppliers aren't available for deliveries, and the majority of people have already planned short breaks or longer vacations. Our Bristol operational site would be running with skeleton staff only, therefore not creating a great impression for the Chairman's visit. Furthermore, all internal services e.g. in-house catering, reception and meeting support – would be on holiday.

Also, our Chairman had requested all members of the UK Board to attend. Therefore, Maria was required to recall all UK Board members to join the meeting with our Global VIPs – in other words, the UK public holiday weekend was cancelled. This was particularly unfortunate for myself as I was scheduled to be on a family holiday in Turkey!

Maria managed all aspects of the event, and arranged travel for myself from Turkey, back to the UK for 2 nights, with another outbound flight back to Turkey (post the meetings) to enable me to re-join my family who were still on vacation. Maria found solutions to all issues, thought through all problems logically and methodically, and produced a meticulously planned Itinerary. Maria sourced pre-ordered food items from the US, sourced a specialist chef, and personally designed and commissioned a bespoke gift item with Bristol Blue Glass. She also sacrificed her Bank Holiday weekend to manage the event.

The visiting company VIPs were extremely satisfied, very appreciative and the meeting and the site visit were highly productive. And most of all, my children were ecstatic as I managed to collect their swimming goggles from the UK, which they had forgotten to pack, and hand deliver them to Turkey!"

John Croft, President and Founder, Elevate Services
London, UK

"I had struggled with my previous two PAs, and each had been with me for just a short period of time, as neither worked out. The HR team put my next PA through a series of 'what would you do if John was going to a meeting and stranded by the roadside' kind of questions. I said at the time that I thought that kind of questioning was unnecessary, but I was quickly proved wrong.

A couple of months later, I was stranded in New York, during the Icelandic volcanic ash incident of 2010. On the fourth day I got a call from my wife, telling me that our eight year old son had been involved in an accident, and was in the back of an ambulance going to Accident and Emergency. I was sick with worry and called my PA, Maria Fuller, to see if she could figure out a way to get me home – despite the fact there had been a global ban on international flights for some days now. She somehow managed to find me a seat on a flight that had opened up that very hour to Casablanca, from where I could take a boat across the sea from North Africa to France, and then a train across France and back to London.

By the time I landed at Casablanca, she had managed to find me a flight, that had just that moment, been allowed to operate from there to London and got me the last seat on it. So I was home with my son within 24 hours!

This 'above and beyond' approach, to a situation that was far more personal than business, is what sets apart the truly fantastic PA from one who is just there to do a job".

2

So, you want to be a PA?

So, you want to be a PA?

What's in this chapter?

There are very exciting times ahead for PAs, and if this is your career choice – congratulations! So, you want to be a PA? If you do - you are about to embark on a journey where the sky is the limit, and opportunities are in abundance. In this chapter, we'll look at the scope of the PA role in more detail, the skills required to do the job successfully, and review a snapshot of fabulous PA recruitment ads. Subtitles in this chapter include:

* Today's PA
* Considering the PA role as a career
* How do I get started as a PA?
* Jobs for the boys
* What makes a great PA?
* Hard and soft skills
* Golden opportunities

Today's PA

In today's tough business climate – one thing is for certain, every FTSE 100 company executive has a personal assistant to support them. Furthermore, every President or EVP presiding over a Dow Jones listed corporation – has a personal assistant at their side, and so does every individual who has ever appeared on the Forbes rich list. Why? Because behind every great man or woman - there is a great PA.

Today's successful business leaders, and entrepreneurs, operate in a ruthless and rapidly changing environment. To stay ahead of their game, leaders rely upon their own internal support network, which consist of company board members, non-executive directors and consultants. But, the one thing which they all utilise - is the support of their personal assistant. Forget the old fashioned image of a secretary typing letters for her boss, and taking him regular cups of tea, things have gone stratospheric in the world of admin support. PAs are being asked to project manage, run corporate events, book global travel, organise conferences, arrange global webcasts, and organise PR and marketing campaigns. As well as travelling with their executive to support the latest product launch or store opening, manage the CEO's personal household staff or even organise the maintenance of the company yacht!

As companies change and evolve, and technology advances, supporting roles too have developed. Today's PA is tech savvy, a diary management guru and a firm gatekeeper for the high net worth individual. PAs have become management assistants, and so you should not underestimate the scope of the role, or the responsibilities which come with it. Exciting times are ahead for today's PA, and industries are recognising the importance and effectiveness of PAs in business. There has been a shift in the valuation of the role, plus the salary and benefits available for today's PA are increasingly attractive.

So, you want to be a PA?

An article in an American newspaper commented on the meteoric rise of the scope of today's PA:

"In Silicon Valley, a once lowly job with meagre pay is starting to mean big bucks - and quite a bit of influence. It's the golden age of the executive assistant. Highly educated, ambitious young people, most of them women, with off-the-map "soft skills" are seeing an employment boom in the support world.

Executive assistants to CEOs, engineers and even middle managers, at major tech companies, increasingly have their pick of top jobs. Why? Because of a wealthy tech economy, less hierarchical companies, and a cultural shift in how assistants are viewed. Once powerless, the executive assistant is now a gatekeeper, charged with keeping the big man or woman on task.

The EA could be the underappreciated career of the century. The base salary starts around $60,000 (£41,000) and goes up fast from there... to as much as $200,000, (£138,000) plus bonuses and equity".

Source: USA Today, October 2014

Today's PA role is fast becoming a management support role, a 'business assistant' in its own right, and is a role worth seriously considering, if you choose to enter today's business world.

Considering the PA role as a career

I am one of the many, successful PAs, who fell into the role without making it a conscious career decision. The role of a PA was not even mentioned by my careers advisor, and only the title of 'Secretary' was listed in the 'Career Options Directory 1991' when I was leaving school. Had todays PA role been available in 1991, I would have chosen it, without a hesitation. Not knowing what I really wanted to do, and after dropping out of 2 college courses in quick succession, I started out learning the basics of office administration. I completed training courses in RSA 1 & 2 Typewriting, and RSA 1 & 2 Word Processing.

These qualifications allowed me to layout documents correctly, touch type with a reasonable speed (60 wpm), produce letters (there was a lot of letter writing back then!), and understand my way around a word processing package. With those basic office skills, and a respectable set of GCSEs, I launched myself into the 9-5 world and found employment in a local Estate Agency as a Secretary. Twenty two years further down the line, and several training courses later, I am Executive Assistant to the country head of a global outsourcing company. The CEO I support, is responsible for the UK, Ireland and South Africa, with a workforce of 10,000 employees (UK). The company, Teleperformance, is the leading supplier in outsourced customer services - worldwide. I am very proud to support him and to have reached this level in my career.

How did I get there? Hopefully, by sharing my insights with you, through this book, you will understand how to progress your own career - but it hasn't been easy. If you really want to succeed as a PA, you have to personally push for the sought after positions, in the desirable companies. The opportunities do not drop in your lap. However, I have had, overall, a great career.

I've managed many corporate events, which is always hard work but great fun, met lots of interesting people, worked in some fabulous office locations in London and Bristol, and attended some amazing corporate parties over the years. I've managed, and attended, numerous corporate events including management retreats in Provence, horse-racing in Windsor, golf at Celtic Manor, shooting in Scotland, private dining at the Gherkin, London and arranged many conferences, exhibitions and away days.

I've been privy to a great deal of confidential information, including company acquisitions, £50M business deals, multi million pound business wins and worked alongside some of the top business brains in legal, financial and outsourcing services. In the executives I have supported, I have seen brilliance, entrepreneurs, innovators and business leaders – and it's been a privilege and an education to work alongside them.

Whilst being a PA can be challenging, interesting, rewarding, stressful, enjoyable and demanding (all at the same time), it's a career choice which is always evolving, and in today's current business climate, it is a highly sought after position – steadily gaining in recognition. As a PA, you will work closely with 1 or 2 business executives. Providing that individual with efficient, business support, and constantly improving their day to day efficiencies within the business. Supporting an executive, (and this is a support role), your focus is on the executive and whatever you can do to maximise their working 'uptime' and minimise any 'downtime' and disruption to their working day. You become the 'go to' person for that individual, you are master at what you do, you can acquire anything they ask for, and solve any problem you are asked to solve.

PAs are multi-taskers, organisational wizards, unflappable admins, and the right hand to the business executive. PAs are not in the limelight, they are behind the scenes, supporting the leading man or woman. If you personally are looking to shine under a spotlight, then this isn't the role for you. Your manager leads and you support – but that doesn't mean you cannot progress and grow the role in other directions. Many PAs are handed projects to manage, on behalf of their manager, or given additional responsibilities e.g. event management or travel co-ordination. The variety of the PA role is vast, and sometimes it's dependent upon what you make it. The interesting element to a PAs role, is that we can get involved in other areas of the business, if required. There isn't a rigid job description or expectation, it can be flexible and fluid.

I have found being a PA to be a very interesting, and varied, career choice. I have travelled, moved sectors, started small and then gradually worked my way up to the larger corporates. I find the role is unique, and definitely rewarding. I thoroughly recommend the role of 'PA' to those considering a career in business support. It allows you room to grow, develop and find your niche in the world of business support professionals.

How do I get started as a PA?

Getting into the PA sector isn't as easy as firing off your CV to 100s of prospective employers, and hoping one of them will bite. If you are seriously contemplating a career as a PA, you'll need to understand which qualities are required in order to succeed, and what a prospective employer is looking for.

What are the entry level requirements to do the job well, and where do your skills and experience match? Which qualifications are desirable, and which IT courses should you undertake to boost your credentials? Which interpersonal skills do you possess, or recognise need further development? Should you embark on a general business studies course, or a business degree before applying for vacancies? Perhaps a language course is appealing to you, if you have your sights set on an international position. Have you considered a sector specific course e.g. a legal secretarial diploma, a medical administration diploma or a bilingual assistant course? Decisions, decisions, decisions!

There is a plethora of administrative, business and personal assistant courses available in today's market place, and knowing which course to enrol on is a challenge in itself. But before you commit yourself to the latest course in the market place, there are several decisions to be made. Consider, which sector or industry appeals to you e.g. public or private, are you seeking employment in a large corporate, a small family business or local government? Furthermore, consider what kind of department or environment appeals to you e.g. finance, business development, education, customer services, human resources, operations, a private household, or supporting an entrepreneur. Chapter 3 'Choosing your Career Path' walks you through all the different sectors, and PA specialisms in further detail. When you have reached a decision, then and only then, should you shortlist your training requirements, in order to achieve your end goal.

Touch typing is a skill which I use every day. If you don't know how to touch type – learn to – fast. You will become more efficient and effective in your role as a PA. It's an invaluable skill to have.

One way into a desirable company is to secure a temporary assignment or short term contract. For many, it is an ideal way to gain temporary employment within that impressive tech company, that you've had your eye on e.g. Facebook, Ebay or Google. Even if the permanent PA position you really desire is not yet available, taking a temporary PA role - is a way in. Employers always look favourably on temp to perm applications, and if you have impressed your manager whilst in a temp role, and enjoy the job, you can express your interest to join on a permanent basis.

One way to test the water and decide if being a PA is right for you, is to enrol with an agency and embark on temporary work placements or short term contract roles. This way you get your foot in the door, can try different departments and sectors, and are under no obligation to stay, if you're not enjoying it.

Jobs for the boys

Yes, it's true, the position of a secretary or personal assistant used to be thought of as a 'predominantly female' role, but now men are breaking down those barriers. And why not? There is no reason why a PA role should be stereotyped as a female job. And, equally, no reason why a man should not have a successful and rewarding career as a PA. So what has brought about this recent change? It's a combination of different factors. The role itself has evolved considerably over the years, from a traditional typist/secretary to today's multi functioning business assistant. It's become more appealing to both genders, and has attracted the attention of young professionals and graduates, seeking an opening into the world of business. An article published in a UK newspaper reported:

"Men are applying for PA roles more frequently, and that change is due partly, to the highest rate of graduate unemployment since records began, and the growing awareness that salaries, for corporate PAs, can reach £75,000 a year in London". *Source: The Observer, October 2013*

In London, recruitment consultants are seeing an ever-increasing number of men interested in PA or secretarial posts. David Morel, MD of Tiger Recruitment advised:

"Out of the 1,000 candidates we've registered in the past 12 months, around 200 are male. It is increasing the whole time. Since 2011, the numbers have been doubling each year, and most of them are ambitious graduates".
Source: The Guardian, October 2013

Certain employers are actively promoting the PA role to male candidates. In particular, the financial services provider, Barclays, now employs several male PAs at a senior level. Barclays said it was committed to encouraging male applicants for PA and admin roles.

"It is important to us that we offer everyone – regardless of their gender – the same opportunities to be successful," said a Barclay's spokesperson.
Source: The Guardian, October 2013

The influx of males into the PA environment, is definitely a trend which is replicating around the world. For example, in the Middle East, it is not uncommon for the majority of PAs within an organization to be male. Globally, women still hold the lion's share of PA positions, but the balance is tipping, as men become to realise the management responsibilities, status and rewards of the profession.

What makes a great PA?

For the moment, let's consider the genetic make-up of a PA. What makes a great PA? Do you need to be degree educated? Privately educated? Multi lingual? A whizz with numbers? Do you need general business experience and a grasp of commerce? In my experience, successful PAs, who have held senior positions, have done so with differing levels of educational achievement.

There isn't a recognized educational route to success, and that's why achieving success as a PA is in everybody's grasp. There are top level PAs with and without degree level educations. There are successful PAs who sailed through college and those who didn't. There are PAs who planned their career whilst at school, and those who fell into the position by accident. But what's really required to succeed, is a good balance of skills, determination, and bucket loads of common sense. An armoury of higher education certificates will get your foot through the door, but if you cannot multitask, prioritise and deal with the unexpected, you will fall from grace quite rapidly.

Shorthand – save yourself a heap of time and don't enrol on a shorthand course. In my 22 years as a PA, I haven't learnt shorthand and it hasn't hindered me – once. Focus on touch typing and if you're asked to minute a meeting – take your laptop with you and take the minutes down direct to keyboard. Save your typed notes on your desktop, and worry about the formatting later. Why would you learn a mystical language such as shorthand, which no-one else in your office understands? If you take minutes using shorthand – you effectively take minutes twice. Once in shorthand script, and a second time, when you translate your notes into typescript. Why would you do a job twice? It's an outdated skill and don't let training providers tell you differently.

Concentrate on improving your 'words per minute' touch typing count. There are several free web based tests for this – have a go and check your score with your friends or colleagues! Try www.speedtypingonline.com/typing-test for your existing typing speed and accuracy. If you are super-fast – share your results on Twitter #howtobeapa.

Hard and soft skills

One route to success is to develop your 'hard', and 'soft', skills in equal measures. Employers look for a combination of hard and soft skills, when interviewing prospective candidates. Hard skills are the technical skills which allow you to do your job. For example, being a competent IT user and understanding various software applications. These skills are generally taught through colleges, and training providers, and upon completion a qualification or certificate is awarded. As a PA the hard skills can include: a good standard of general education, computer literacy, MS office competency, business administration, audio transcription, minute taking, document production, touch typing with good typing speeds and travel management. Whilst successful study of training courses can provide you with the hard skills employers are looking for, ultimately, the ability to succeed as a PA is also dependent upon your soft skills.

Soft skills are the skills which are mostly unquantifiable, the skills which are interpersonal and make up your personal qualities and attitudes. Soft skills, also known as 'emotional intelligence', are your character traits and insights, and they enhance your interaction with other individuals. They define who you are and include your habits, how you connect with other people and how you read situations and build relationships. Of course, you can develop some of your soft skills with experience throughout your life, but if your personality type isn't comfortable with certain situations you will face as a PA e.g. taking criticism, receiving instruction, being given new projects without notice, working to tight deadlines and staying until the job is complete, then the role is not for you.

 Can you identify soft skills v hard skills? Read the workplace scenario over, and complete the soft skills v hard skills table on the following pages.

30

So, you want to be a PA?

A typical working day for a PA will require you to draw upon your hard, and soft skills, in equal measures. Let's look at a particular scenario. For example, you work for a large financial services company and support the Director of Global Investments. The monthly board meeting is next week. You are required to complete the monthly investment report by collating the figures across 4 teams, produce PowerPoint slides, import graphs and tables from an Excel file, and submit the report to the CEO's PA in advance. Your deadline is 1500.

In addition your manager has just asked you to minute his team meeting which commences at 1300, organize lunch for the attendees at short notice, and find a meeting room. You're fully aware that all meetings rooms are showing as reserved on the system, plus your personal diary shows you've agreed to meet your friend Michael for lunch today. Your phone is ringing and upon answering it, Reception advise you that a client, Mr Hobbs, (a High Net Worth Individual - who is notoriously difficult) has arrived unexpectedly and is waiting in Reception to see your line manager. The current time is 1100 and you know your boss is interviewing a candidate in Room 3. Arrgghhh!!! Do you recognize the skill types involved in order to complete these tasks successfully? Let's see if you can match the skills types required, to the individual tasks.

 Review the skill types below. Match the skills types you think are required, to complete the various tasks. Use the blank table overleaf to record your answers.

Hard Skills	
Administration	Numeracy
Diary management	Budgetary control
Document layout and production	IT literacy
Minute taking	General office skills
MS Office competency	Proof reading
Word processing	Touch typing
Soft Skills	
Ability to read body language	Problem solver
Ability to work to deadline	Listening skills
Assertiveness	Courtesy
Confidence	Meeting management
Dealing with the unexpected	Self-motivation
Flexibility	Patience
Negotiation	Team player
Networking	Good communicator
Prioritisation	Diplomacy
Professionalism	Ability to work under pressure
Time management	

So, you want to be a PA?

Hard skills v soft skills – the tasks:

TASK	HARD SKILLS	SOFT SKILLS
Collate the monthly board report data and submit to deadline		
Minute the team meeting		
Organize lunch and a meeting room		
Reschedule your personal lunch appointment		
Dealing with the unexpected client 'Mr Hobbs'		

Can you see now, how important it is to understand and develop hard and soft skills in equal measure? Hard and soft skills are drawn upon frequently, when working through the tasks. Failing to value the importance of both, throughout your career, could be a potential barrier, and will undoubtedly hamper your progression. How do your answers compare? See page 45 for the results.

Employers also value candidates demonstrating their soft skills during the interview process, and its worthwhile remembering this when faced with a 'what would you do if xyz' question is asked. Demonstrate your emotional intelligence, and provide examples of your soft skills at interview.

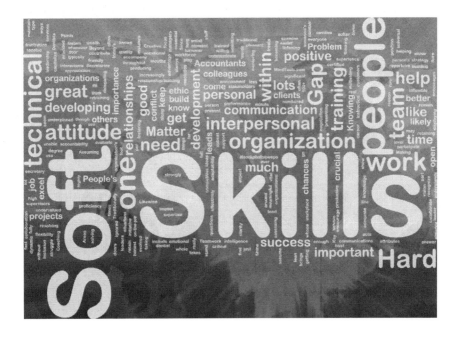

Golden opportunities

A quick search on the internet will reveal a multitude of PA vacancies, around the world. This is useful, not only when searching for a new position, but also exploring the scope of opportunities in existence, and the potential for your own development. The snapshot of genuine advertisements which follow, demonstrates the variety of positions on offer. From supporting the Chairman of a luxury brand in London, to assisting an individual and his family in Monaco, or working for the CEO of an investment company in Dubai – the range of PA positions available is truly fantastic.

Of course, not all positions advertised are so glamourous! But what's the harm in letting yourself dream and setting your sights on the end goal? With experience and determination – these opportunities are not beyond your reach.

PA to Marketing Director / Media to $75K
Including a Super Package
Sydney

• Work for a brand you will be truly proud of

• Fabulous city location   • Fantastic Boss

The Company: we are recruiting for a role that is unfortunately going to bring out the green eyed monster with your peers, a PA for a successful high profile company. The vacancy is due to an internal promotion and you will assist with supporting the Marketing Director. This person is a well-respected player in the industry; fast paced, direct, two days never the same are all words that spring to mind when talking about his work ethic.

The Role: Day to day you will ensure the smooth running of his day. This will mean getting involved in all the usual PA duties — diary management, coordinating travel (domestic and international), expenses, gate keeping, some personal errands....all sounds pretty normal but working in great offices at an impressive global brand.

Personal Assistant to Real Estate CEO/Owner
(Full-time)
San Diego, California

Successful real estate executive/owner and single dad seeks personal assistant to manage all aspects of personal, family and professional life. Responsibilities include maintaining personal and business schedules, making/monitoring travel arrangements, management of personal residences including oversight of domestic staff, coordination of children's activities and schedules, personal shopping and errand running, etc. Ideal candidate has professional business background coupled with enthusiasm for taking on any and all personal tasks necessary to free high performing executive to focus on his professional responsibilities. North San Diego County resident a plus; flexible work hours are a necessity.

Salary: Competitive salary coupled with generous benefits package.

So, you want to be a PA?

Executive Assistant (Chairman)

Luxury Group

From £60,000 to £70,000 per year + + bonus + top package

London - Permanent Full time

Business Assistant (Chairman) Luxury Group - W1. A top opportunity has arisen for a polished and educated (degree preferred) Executive Assistant to support this HNW Chairman of an international luxury group. You will have supported someone of this standing in the past on both a personal and business level and have the commitment and knowledge to liaise on an international level. High level meetings, travel + itineraries to the USA and Europe and daily liaison with household staff in the US and UK + drivers etc. Flexibility on hours (and maybe some travel) will be needed as this is a true career EA role and requires out of hours support. Wonderful offices and top team in the London HQ (80)+. Resilient, confident and professional this is a top role for a top EA who is dedicated, highly organised and able to bring many skills to the table. Top package.

LEGAL PA / EXECUTIVE ASSISTANT – CITY

From £45,000 to £45,000 per year

London Permanent Full time

Rare opportunity for a Legal PA who has worked at executive assistant level, and who would relish a full Legal PA function working alongside the international managing partner of this leading City law firm.

He is looking for someone who has worked at senior level, who is used to managing all aspects of an extensive travel itinerary, overseeing all incoming and outgoing communication, assisting with marketing support and arrangements for events, as well as organising personal holidays and payment of bills etc. It's a great opportunity for a Legal PA to take on a role which offers enormous scope to exercise your organising skills and initiative.

Salary 70000 to 80000 Euros

Location Monaco

Contract Type Permanent

Job Role PA

Description

A sensational new role has arisen supporting a hugely wealthy and charming individual and his family in Monaco.

An involved and varied role, you will be supporting in both a business and personal capacity, and will therefore be involved in every aspect of the family's lives; personal shopping, managing bank accounts, arranging luxury holidays, coordinating board meetings, extensive travel arrangements and overseeing staff across a portfolio of properties.

This is a highly exciting role for a switched on, dynamic, proactive and experienced PA looking for a meaty and fast-paced role.

If this sounds like you, apply now!

EA TO UBER HNW Salary 60000 to 90000 GBP

Location London

Contract Type Permanent

Job Role Executive Assistant

Industry Sector Banking and Finance

Description

Are you quite simply the best EA in town? Do you live to work, rather than work to live? Do you thrive under pressure, rise to a challenge and enjoy solving problems? Do you see a team as greater than the sum of its parts? I am looking for an extremely intelligent, switched on EA of the highest calibre to support this HNW individual, in this newly founded Family Office. Working as a senior member of his team, you will be facilitating every aspect of his life on both the business and personal side. You will need to be a chameleon and jack of all trades, turning your hand to anything that is required of you, constantly juggling priorities and always striving for perfection.

Attention to detail is paramount as there is no room for error – the standard of your work must be meticulous. Acting as a gate-keeper, you will mentor, manage and guide junior PAs, to whom you can delegate and offload. This is not for the faint-hearted – you will need to be tough, thick-skinned and resilient, giving everything for minimal thanks or recognition. That said, in return you will be rewarded financially at an amazing level. Is this you....? Apply now!

EA to High Net Worth Individual
Hours: 9-6pm
Salary: $95,000-120,000
New York

Job description

Seeking a highly qualified Executive Personal Assistant - to work for a high net worth individual. This role is located in the office of the asset management firm where the CEO is based.

Responsibilities:

All personal assistant duties: (manage multiple homes, interact with the family, send out invitations, plan personal events, vacations, etc.)

Coordinate all logistics of international and domestic travel (detailed itineraries and agenda).

Maintain calendars; organize and schedule appointments.

Filter through high volume of telephone calls, email and mail with responsibility for very timely follow up.

Draft correspondence and other documents.

Liaise with household staff as needed.

Requirements

10 years of administrative/personal assistant experience required.

Creative Director of Luxury French Fashion House needs an Assistant!
Salary 28000 to 32000 Euros
Location London
Contract Type Permanent
Job Role PA
Industry Sector Luxury Brands/Goods

This is a once in a life time chance to take the next step working within luxury fashion. A London based, hugely successful French Fashion House is looking for an assistant to support the PA to the Creative Director in this busy, creative, diverse and successful environment. Supporting the creative director with business and personal duties (as delegated by her PA) you will be looking after travel, diaries, press, studio assistants, liaising with the creative team, working with images, running errands, travelling and so much more. This is a frenetic and demanding environment and the successful candidate must have strong PA skills, fantastic IT and the ability to create order amongst chaos.

Priorities, demands and duties are ever changing and you will have the flexibility to deal with this, and the confidence to deal with some of the most senior people in the business. As an ambassador for the Creative Director you will be impeccably stylish, bright, confident, brand aware and inspired by the luxury industry. Not for the faint hearted, this role requires someone dedicated and hardworking who is willing to give 110%. Candidates should be aware that you will be required to travel between London and Paris. If this sounds like you then we want to hear from you now!!

Executive Assistant to CEO
Dubai, UAE
Salary: AED 180,000 – 250,000

The Role

We are currently looking for an experienced Executive Assistant to support the CEO of an Investment company in Dubai.

Responsibilities will include but are not limited to:

- Represent the CEO and the organization in a professional manner in person, in telephone conversations, and in written correspondences at all times.
- Maintain the CEOs appointment schedule by planning and scheduling meetings, conferences, events and travel.
- Drafting letters and documents; collecting and analysing information; initiating telecommunications.
- Attending meetings with the CEO in order to take minutes.
- Order office supplies when required.
- Preparing PowerPoint presentations and reports.
- Greeting the VIPs.
- Filing of confidential documents and keeping information updated.
- Arranging company events/meetings.
- Liaising with management team in regards to business developments.
- Participate in brainstorming sessions for various projects.
- Act as the gatekeeper for the CEO.
- Assist with general office administrative tasks as needed.

Personal Assistant

Salary: $100,000/year

Additional Benefits: Healthcare and housing provided

Vacation: 6 weeks

Location: Northern California (5 months), Uruguay (3-4 months), Colorado (4-6 weeks)

Description: Must be fluent in Spanish

A couple is looking for a personal assistant to travel with them and manage some of their daily affairs. The position will report 80% to the female of the couple and 20% to the male. Candidate needs to be highly organized and will need to coordinate duties with other staff members (inc. male's private secretary of owned business). Such tasks might include coordinating the couples travel, keeping up with calendars of guests, and communicating with other staff members. This person will organize and coordinate guest "programs" as various locations and ensure guest's needs are anticipated for and fulfilled. Candidate should have knowledge of fine wines and food. Responsible for dinner parties, personal appointments, transportation needs (of couple, guests, and business affairs). Relationship with couple will be friendly and informal; in an exaggerated example the perfect situation would be that this person would have almost no interaction with the principals because everything is running as it should be.

Complete your own online research for PA vacancies. List what attracts you to particular roles, and in which sectors. Create a 'shopping list' for your ideal job.

Executive Assistant (Board Level) Saudi Arabia

£60,000 - £70,000 - Tax Free

A leading Energy company based in Saudi Arabia. £60,000 - £70,000 (Tax Free) + benefits with housing allowance, travel allowance and tax free savings. Relocation package for the candidate only, including accommodation, VISAs, travel.

You will be living within an ex-pat community in a typically beautiful complex with swimming pool, gym and other luxuries. Situated in Western Saudi Arabia with easy travel into Bahrain. An excellent opportunity to live tax free in a beautiful country.

Professional and experienced Board Level Executive Assistant, enthusiastic, flexible and enjoy a challenging and fast-paced office environment, to work for our corporate and executive management team.

Oil and gas industry experience would be an added bonus, but candidate selection will mainly be based upon personal skills and experience working at Senior Board Level.

Duties and Responsibilities include, but are not limited to:

• Extensive diary management. • Arranging travel, both within Kingdom and international. • Itinerary preparation and visa paperwork, if necessary. • Managing expense claims. • Ensure office is running smoothly so management can concentrate on core business activities. • Perform highly confidential secretarial and administrative duties. • Composition, editing and review of confidential correspondence. • Preparing board packs and working at board level is essential.

We welcome applications from all suitably qualified candidates. Note that relocation assistance is unavailable for spouses, partners or other family members.

Minimum Requirements:

The candidate will have a number of years Executive Assistant experience supporting at Board level with a stable CV. The position requires outstanding typing skills, a minimum of 55 wpm, with 85% accuracy. Shorthand is desirable.

The candidate will combine excellent English writing and speaking skills with initiative and the ability to thrive under pressure. The candidate will also be proficient with Microsoft computer applications, such as Word, Excel and PowerPoint.

Of course, there are less demanding PA positons available. Positions which perhaps you would feel more comfortable with, during the early part of your career. There are also part time opportunities, job shares, covering maternity leaver's absence and fixed term contracts. The more experience you have, the more opportunities will be available to you. As PAs we continue to learn throughout our career, whilst continuing with our own personal development. So, you definitely want to be a PA – but which sector or specialism is attractive to you? Chapter 3 'Choosing your career path' will help you to do just that.

Hard skills v soft skills – the answers:

TASK	HARD SKILLS	SOFT SKILLS
Collate the monthly board report data and submit to deadline	Word processing Touch typing Document layout IT literacy MS Office competency Proof reading	Work to deadline Self-motivation Assertiveness Confidence Courtesy Time management Good communicator Negotiation Team player Professionalism Ability to work under pressure
Minute the team meeting	Minute taking General office skills Document production Touch typing Administration Proof reading	Dealing with the unexpected Flexibility Good listener Good communicator Ability to read body language Team player Confidence Meeting management Professionalism Time management
Organize lunch and a meeting room	Numeracy Budgetary control Diary management MS Office competency	Ability to work under pressure Flexibility Assertiveness Meeting management Negotiation Ability to work to deadline Problem solver Good communicator Prioritisation Patience

Reschedule your personal lunch appointment	Diary management	Patience Flexibility Courtesy Professionalism
Dealing with the unexpected client 'Mr Hobbs'	Diary management	Dealing with the unexpected Problem solver Good communicator Professionalism Diplomacy Assertiveness Prioritisation Confidence Ability to work under pressure Professionalism

3

Choosing your Career Path

What's in this chapter?

In order to establish and progress your career path, we will explore the different sectors, and industries available to you - as a PA. There are a multitude of working environments worth considering, from supporting a finance director in a retail company to a CEO of a large pharmaceutical company, a hotel operational director, a leader of a global brand or an uber high net worth individual.

We will also take time to understand the different job titles in existence in the PA market, and take a more, in-depth, look at the key elements of the PA role. A personal assistant requires many skills, in order to do his or her job successfully, but the particular skillset required can be dependent upon your chosen career path. Certain industries require specific, work related skills, e.g. law (legal transcription), medical environments (medical terminology), or property (understanding contracts and searches). You will need to understand which skills are specific to your chosen career path, and which skills you need to learn and develop.

On the upside, PA skills are easily transferable between sectors, which is a huge positive. Once the basic, core, skills are mastered, and with a certain degree of work experience behind you, you can change sectors, or industries, without too much difficulty. This provides you with greater career options, and endless possibilities. In this chapter we will review career paths in more detail, by looking at:

- Job titles explained
- The key elements of the PA role
- Personal qualities and PA super skills
- Which sector: public, private or not for profit?
- My career path and industry insights
- Getting your foot on the ladder to C suite

Job titles explained

As the recruitment advertisements in the previous chapter demonstrated, the job titles used in PA recruitment can vary widely. It is important to understand the definitions and responsibilities, as it will aid with career choices, manage expectations of the role itself, and define career progression opportunities.

The variety of job titles used, across business support roles, has evolved to reflect the business environment, the level of seniority, and the sector in which the role is based. Globally, there are some variances on titles, however, the titles listed below are most commonly used, and translate across the continent.

In alphabetical order, the most commonly used job titles for today's business support/PA roles are:

Business Support Job Titles	
Administrator	Bilingual PA
C- Level Assistant	Celebrity PA
Executive Assistant	Legal Secretary/PA
Medical Secretary/PA	Office Assistant
Office Manager	Personal Assistant
PA to HNWI	Receptionist
Secretary	Team PA
Team Secretary	Typist/Audio typist
Virtual Assistant	

A definition of each role follows:

Administrator: a person responsible for the performance or management of administrative tasks. Largely involving supporting a department with invoicing, daily administration, processing documentation, and supporting with finance administration. Managing office systems, inputting data, maintaining databases and filing.

Bilingual PA: a PA with specialist language skills e.g. they communicate using English plus one or more foreign language. Excellent communication is required, confidence, and fluency in 2 languages (both written and spoken). These roles are often found in global and international organisations, and can command higher salaries due to the level of expertise.

C-Level Assistant: an American term but one that is becoming more widely used. C-level, or C-suite, describes high ranking executives who have reached the level of Chief Executive Officer, Chief Operating Officer or Chief Financial Officer etc. Basically, any board level position beginning with the title 'Chief'. Executives who hold C-level positions are typically considered the most powerful and influential members of an organisation; consequently, they make higher-stakes decisions, their workload is more demanding, the hours worked are considerable, and they earn relatively high salaries. The C-Level Assistant is an executive assistant providing support to a C-level, or C-suite level, business executive.

Celebrity PA: a PA who supports a celebrity. The Celebrity PA is the 'right hand' of the employer, and is responsible for the scheduling and structuring of the employer's private, social, and business calendars. Arranging all public appearances, co-ordinating travel arrangements, catering and maintaining daily itineraries. Often involved with managing the household, this is very different from a corporate environment, and very hands on. The Celebrity PA works extremely closely with their 'celeb', helps protect the brand, often supports with social media communications, such as Twitter, supports with press engagement, and will travel when necessary with their celebrity. Confidentiality is paramount, as well as the ability to deal with potentially difficult individuals.

Executive Assistant: a PA supporting a senior level executive, with additional responsibilities e.g. board administration, project and event management, marketing or PR. EAs are pro-active in their support, they prompt their executive to action tasks when necessary, and act on their executive's behalf when required. Often attending meetings, independent of their executive, and having line management for admin support roles. EAs will be found at the higher levels of the organisation structure. Not restricted to supporting just 1 executive, EAs commonly support 2-3.

Legal Secretary/PA: a Secretary or PA working in a legal environment. In addition to the standard secretarial and administrative support required, Legal Secretaries must have excellent spoken and written English, and be fast and accurate, audio and copy typists. Commonly supporting multiple fee earners, and lawyers with time recording, invoicing, document production and formatting. Completing legal searches, diary and travel management, and document filing/storage. There are many different areas of law and practice, such as conveyancing, tax, litigation, finance, construction, family and criminal law. Legal Secretaries can specialise within individual areas of law, and such expertise is considered to be highly desirable by international city law firms.

Medical Secretary/PA: a Secretary or PA working in a medical environment. Medical secretaries provide support to hospitals and doctors, they also support health service managers, consultants, and medical researchers. This can be in the public or private sector. Medical secretaries must have excellent standards of spoken and written English, an understanding of relevant medical terminology, audio and copy typing skills, diary management, and the ability to deal professionally and confidentially, with patient enquiries.

Office Assistant: similar to an 'Administrator' but completing tasks for the wider office team e.g. post, office deliveries, office consumables, dealing with enquiries, supporting the office team with their administration requirements, and contributing to the smooth running of the office.

Office Manager: a management position - responsible for organising all of the administrative activities that facilitate the smooth running of an office. The scope of the role, and responsibility, ultimately depends on the size of the 'office' but the general remit includes: co-ordinating the different functions of the office e.g. admin support, payroll, reception, catering, facilities, and dealing with general enquiries. Line managing support staff, implementing and improving office processes, desk moves, new hardware and new starter set ups. Office managers work closely with facilities teams to ensure that the office environment is the best it can be. An office manager will strive to run the most efficient and productive office environment, whilst meeting all health and safety requirements.

Personal Assistant: a person who provides business support to 1 or 2 business executives. A PA proactively supports their busy executive's working life and will manage their diary, co-ordinate meetings, co-ordinate travel, be the gate keeper, and act as deputy when the executive is unavailable. PAs also produce complex documents such as PowerPoint presentations, build Excel databases, and format lengthy Word documents. PAs provide the 'point of contact' in larger organisations, when their executive is often busy travelling or with clients.

PA to HNWI: a PA to a HNWI (high net worth individual) supports an affluent private business person, with liquid assets in excess of £1M. HNWIs are entrepreneurs, philanthropists, successful board level directors, and C-suite executives. They are business founders, investors, international business travellers, and have multiple homes. Often supporting with the private household, as well as several business interests, this can be a 24-7 role, but with the opportunity to travel. A PA to a HNWI can be requested to manage the private art collection, customise a luxury car with Swarovski crystals, organise the family ski-ing holiday in Verbier, or co-ordinate the private jet! Often HNWIs have a team of private staff to support them, which are co-ordinated by the PA.

Receptionist: the 'front of house' in office support. Receptionists meet and greet clients, operate the switchboard, arrange couriers, deal with post, manage visitor registration, and support with health and safety requirements in the office. They also manage meeting room bookings, cab reservations, order catering for in-house lunches, and support with beverages for visitors. Receptionists are the face of the company, and must have a good rapport with visitors, always presenting a courteous and professional image, whilst ensuring the visitors' experience is professional and productive.

Secretary: a term used less commonly in today's job descriptions, as roles and skills have evolved from the historical office 'Secretary' position. Today's Secretary provides general office support, including audio and copy typing, document formatting, document production, and administrative duties such as expense and invoice processing, and answering calls.

Team PA: similar to the role of PA, but supporting a wider team of managers (approx. 4-6). As the role supports numerous managers in the business, the level of support awarded to each manager proportionately reduces. The Team

PA will concentrate on diary management and document production, together with expense processing, administration and booking meetings. The Team PA often responds to work requests initiated by people in the team, rather than having the time, or the opportunity, to pro-actively recognise what every individual needs.

Team Secretary: an office employee who supports multiple individuals, in a secretarial capacity.

Typist/Audio Typist: this role focuses on the transcription of either the spoken, or written word into a typed format. The typing of hand written notes, or re-typing of printed documentation is known as 'copy typing'. Transcribing from audio and digital sound files is known as 'audio typing'. Digital transcription uses specialist software, so typists must be familiar with the methods/devices used, and the process involved. Fast and accurate touch typing skills are required, together with good levels of grammar and business English. Typists can specialise in legal, or medical environments, or anywhere which has its own recognised terminology. Document formatting skills are also required.

Virtual Assistant: an experienced PA or EA who completes freelance commissions for private clients. A Virtual Assistant is generally self-employed, and provides professional administrative, technical, or creative assistance to clients, remotely from a home office. Virtual Assistants have multiple clients, and manage their own workflow, time and fee structure. VAs can support executives who are based all over the world, as the majority of work is remote and online.

A new job title, which is starting to emerge, is that of '**Business Assistant**'. Business assistants are gradually appearing in job advertisements, job searches and being cited in the media. Originating from the US, this job title more accurately reflects what a senior level PA or EA does. It adds gravitas to the role and elevates it to management status. Business assistants are respected members of management teams, and are pivotal in supporting senior executives to be even more successful. Often involving project management, the responsibilities of the Business assistant role has achieved recognition in the workplace, and deservedly so.

 Which job title and description is the most appealing to you? What is it you most like about that particular role? Do you have the skills required to do the job, or do you recognise areas for personal development?

The key elements of the PA role

For ease of consistency, I am using the job title 'PA' throughout this book. The job title 'PA' is still the most commonly used in the market place, however, the information provided in 'How to be a PA' is relevant across all the different PA sectors and specialisms.

A PAs responsibilities are broad, you could be formatting the monthly sales report at 1000, minuting a meeting at 1100, and booking flights to Boston at 1200, but that's the appeal! The variety makes the role interesting. It can be unpredictable, fast paced, demanding and challenging. Who knows what your manager will ask you to action tomorrow? It could be researching a product, organising a client dinner or obtaining prices for venue hire. As a PA, you will give your expert support to whatever task comes your way. Each task must be completed professionally, efficiently and to deadline. You provide the solutions to the problems, the answers to the questions and the order to the chaos! Personal assistant job titles may vary, as we have just discovered, however the key elements of the different PA roles are predominantly the same. A 2014 survey asked a total of 1,275 PAs, working across the UK, how their day-to-day role was split, in terms of work related tasks. Answers below.

The average split of the PAs Day:

Diary management – 37%
Email management – 23%
Travel management – 4%
Note taking and transcribing – 3%
Errands for your boss -1%
HR – 2%
Event management – 3%
Office management – 15%
Other - 12%

Source: The National PA Survey October 2014

Whilst not being a comprehensive summary of the PAs responsibilities, the activities in the table over often fall within a PAs remit.

A PAs Responsibilities

Acting as a representative	Agenda production
Board meeting management	Booking flights
Booking hotels	Booking meeting rooms
Catering co-ordination	Collating meeting reports
Conference organisation	Diary management
Document formatting	Email management
Event management	Expenses admin
External meeting management	Filtering telephone enquiries
Gatekeeper	Global meeting organisation
Greeting visitors	Internal communications
Internal meeting management	Managing your manager's day
Minute taking	Office administration
Office management	Personal errands
PowerPoint presentations	Private driver bookings
Producing correspondence	Rescheduling appointments
Restaurant reservations	Time management
Travel co-ordination	Travel research
Visa applications	

The typing of hand written notes or re-typing of printed documentation is known as **copy typing**. Transcribing from audio and digital sound files is known as **audio typing**.

Personal qualities and PA super skills

So, how can you be sure that you have what it takes to be a successful PA? Have you got the personal qualities, emotional intelligence or traits required to survive in what can be a very fast moving and pressurised environment? Can you take direct instruction from a senior executive and not get in a flap? Are you comfortable with acting as gatekeeper, and not allowing unscheduled calls to be transferred to your boss, even when the caller persists? Could you negotiate meeting room hire costs, when researching for a conference venue, in order to save your company money? As a PA you cannot afford to be shy, hesitant, nervous or disorganised. What you need to demonstrate is confidence, efficiency, professionalism, and the willingness to support your executive.

Being a PA is also about a working partnership, a bit like a marriage. It's a relationship which will have its occasional flare ups but, for the majority of the time, things will go smoothly and pleasantly, as long as you work at it. When you work so closely with someone, there is the potential to clash or disagree, but a successful PA will manage potentially damaging situations, and prevent them from escalating. Once a working relationship is damaged, it makes for a very difficult working environment, and must be avoided at all costs.

PAs can also be the brunt of an executive's temper. Naomi Campbell, the super model, famously threw her mobile phone at her PA, whilst in a fit of anger. Whilst this is not part of the standard job description, **managing difficult situations** is definitely a skill every PA should perfect.

An ability to mind read is also a key asset for any PA. Not available to study in text books, or found on YouTube, this particular PA super skill is developed with experience. A good PA will know intuitively which meeting his or her manager will attend, and which they will decline. They will know when a manager needs reminding of an imminent client meeting, or when to prompt for a particular client report. A PA will know when a pre-meet is required, or a de-brief needs scheduling. We also know when the 1 to 1s have slipped from the diary and need re-instating, and when to suggest a team meeting or team lunch is required, in order to boost morale or celebrate the latest client win.

Mind reading, otherwise known as **'professional intuition',** is a PA super skill which will stand you in good stead, throughout your career, once mastered. Executives often work at such a pace that they don't have time to think through details – a great PA will be intuitive enough to read situations, pre-empt diary disasters, and diplomatically prompt their manager when they have forgotten a requirement or missed a deadline.

Another PA super skill is being the executive's **'eyes and ears'**. This is a slightly controversial skill as PAs do not wish to be perceived as being spies. However, they have a greater visibility in the work place, than their executive who is often away, or who isn't privy to general office conversations. Being the eyes and ears should be used in a positive way – it should not be used regarding office gossip or trivial matters. For example, if a colleague of yours worked exceptionally hard to win an account, including working across a weekend unpaid, but is too modest to mention it – you could advise your boss of your colleague's efforts. Why not? Your executive could publicise the win, congratulate your colleague, and your colleague feels rewarded and noticed. If you don't mention it, your executive may never know and your colleague begins to feel unappreciated.

As 'eyes and ears' you also have a duty to alert your executive to anything which amounts to misconduct. For example, your executive is always out of the office on Fridays, and 2 members of the team always slip out early, around mid-afternoon, and go home. You've overheard your colleagues discussing this, commenting that it's dishonest but it continues to go undetected. As such, it's creating an atmosphere in the office. Your executive is completely unaware.

So tell your executive in confidence – explain the period of time it's been happening for, and that it's becoming an issue in the office. Your executive will thank you for your honesty, confirm you 'did the right thing', and will address the issue, diplomatically, which will improve internal relations.

To understand your personal skill strengths and skill weaknesses, complete the free online assessments on www.nationalcareersservice.direct.gov.uk, search for 'skills health check'.

The ability to **listen**, and to **question**, are also PA super skills. Listening to your executive when they are delegating work, and understanding the instruction first time around, is important. You must listen during meetings, to understand the key elements, and the actions, which you need to minute. Conference calls also require a PA to listen attentively to record any actions, or minutes. Questions – can be asked whenever something is unclear, particularly when your manager is delegating work to you. Don't wait until the next day to clarify a point – ask immediately. Your executive will appreciate your desire to get things right first time.

Ask questions whenever the instruction you've received isn't comprehensive. For example, you've been asked to organise a team meeting next week, off-site, and to send a diary invitation to attendees when it's confirmed. This isn't enough information for you to accurately complete the task. Ask your executive questions to fill in the gaps e.g. what's the budget, what type of venue had they in mind, will this involve evening drinks or dinner afterwards, what kind of catering is appropriate, how close should the venue be to your office location, is there a dress code, does the team need to complete any preparatory work? By asking these questions, you will have established your brief. You will completely understand what it is your executive wants to achieve, you will know your budget, and have an indication of the venue style and location required for this event. You can now complete the task, without interrupting your executive further.

If you hadn't taken the initiative, and refrained from asking such direct questions, you could potentially have gone over budget, selected a venue in the wrong area, and the meeting wouldn't have met your executive's expectations. This would have reflected upon you, personally, and your ability to do your job well.

The ability to **multi-task** and **prioritise** are also very important personal qualities, for obvious reasons. PAs are usually working through many tasks at once, during the day, and you have to regularly re-order and re-prioritise those tasks, due to a more important deadline hitting your desk. Prioritisation is mostly common sense, and comes with experience. If in doubt – ask your executive. Multi-tasking is the ability to juggle various actions, without dropping the ball. Your organisational skills will support your ability to multi task.

The most important PA super skill is the **ability to organise**. Some people are what you would call 'natural organisers', they enjoy the planning and processes involved, and make the practical look easy. Whereas for others, organisational skills are developed and honed, and constantly improved.

The ability to organise covers all aspects of the PA role, from diary management to email management, to meeting co-ordination and travel planning. A good organiser doesn't forget a detail. Every aspect is considered, reviewed, planned and completed. A good organiser will be meticulous in their attention to detail, take pride in their work, and have high standards and expectations.

Your executive relies on this level of detail, and your ability to organise his or her working life. As diaries flex and change throughout the working week, your organisational abilities are drawn upon constantly to keep the moving pieces of the jigsaw, fitting the picture frame. A good organiser will keep abreast of all changes, all demands and all last minute requests, so that everything is covered, nothing is forgotten and everybody has received a reply to their enquiry.

Super PA organisers are in high demand, and will go far with their chosen career path. Consider a global CEO who is flying to 4 different destinations per week, requiring airport transfers, visas, hotels and meeting arrangements. The CEO also requires a client dinner arranging at short notice, a car to pick up his dinner guest, research completed and a biography provided on his dinner guest prior to that engagement. That's a lot of organising, and this is where someone without the personal qualities, and PA super skills, will come unstuck. If you know that you are super organised, never forget a detail, and would relish that kind of itinerary to co-ordinate, then you are on the right road to PA success.

Which sector - public, private or not for profit?

Throughout my career as a PA, I've always worked in the private sector, but I've been employed in several different industries including property, law, print, finance, insurance, investment, and outsourcing. But PA positions are found across all economic sectors. Some sectors will pay more than others, for example, private sector positions invariably pay more, than positions in the public sector. Legal and financial services roles will undoubtedly pay more than positions secured in local government or education. However, if it's an ethical decision, you may prefer to work for the 'not for profit', charitable sector, rather than a large corporate or a profit driven organisation. Let's look at the 3 sectors of public, private and not for profit, in more detail.

How the Economy is split by Sector	
Public Sector	The public sector provides various government services. Employment across the public sector includes opportunities in education, schools, the police, public transport, health care, social services and those working for the government itself e.g. local authority or public funded services.
Private Sector	The private sector is the part of a country's economic system that is run by individuals and companies, rather than the government. Most private sector organisations are run with the intention of making profit. This includes small independent businesses to a large corporate. The private sector includes law firms, financial services, energy companies, tech start-ups, and HNWI individuals. Further industries include construction, media, food, retail, oil and gas, manufacturing and pharmaceuticals, amongst others.
Not for profit Sector	These are non-government organisations which are 'not for profit'. Also known as the voluntary sector, community sector and the third sector. Organisations include

charities, housing associations, mutual societies, cooperatives, trade unions, credit unions, industry associations and sports clubs. Also known as NPO (non-profit organisation), the organisation will use its surplus revenues to further achieve its purpose or mission.

Consider the 3 sectors. Consider your likes and dislikes. Which sector do you find the most attractive? Which sector inspires you and interests you? How does that sector correlate with your career path choice? List all the answers to the above.

Add to bible...

Add your goals to your bible. Which sector you have chosen, which industry you would like to work in, which role is your ideal role and which location. Use this as your reminder and inspiration for where you want to be.

My career path and industry insights

Like many school leavers, I deviated from the career path I had originally chosen, upon leaving school. I began studying for A-levels, but dropped out of sixth form college after 6 months. I embarked on a 2 year Travel and Tourism course, and quit the course after 6 months. My final attempt was to complete a full time Business Management course, which, yes you guessed it, I gave up after 6 months. I came to the conclusion that higher education was not for me! What I did do successfully, was to enrol myself on a few evening classes, including touch typing and word processing. I enjoyed the practical element of producing documents in a professional way, with a high level of accuracy and detail. Following successful completion of the part time secretarial training courses (with excellent results), I updated my CV and started job hunting, for a full time secretarial position.

Your CV is not only evidence of your career history, work experience and qualifications. It's also an example of your document layout skills and formatting. Print a hard copy of your CV, and proof read it, line by line, to ensure 100% accuracy.

My first secretarial position was in the private sector, in an estate agency in the South West of England. I gained work experience in a small office environment (6 staff total), improved my IT skills, and met clients and purchasers on a daily basis. My role was to greet prospective house purchasers as they came into the office, type up house particulars, arrange viewings, and answer the phones. The role was very client facing, I was front of house, and as such expected to jump up from behind my desk, whenever a client or purchaser dropped in. It was an enjoyable role, but my opportunities for growth and promotion were limited, due to the small size of the business. I knew I preferred the private sector over the public or charitable sectors, but hadn't quite found my niche.

From that position, I moved into a legal secretary (conveyancing) position in Exeter, Devon. Supporting 2 partners with their administration needs, completing legal searches and handling telephone enquiries. The role was still in the private sector, but I had moved into a more structured, professional, environment. My position was less client facing, and the office was considerably bigger (50 employees). I enjoyed being in a larger office environment with more people to interact with, and I was impressed with the prestige associated with working for a prominent, county, law firm.

With a hunger for career success, and the desire to further my career outside of the provinces, I headed to London. London, at 20 years of age, was both exciting and daunting in equal measures. I think any capital city is, if you grew up in a less populated location. I moved to London with nothing but my skills, my ambition, and a desire to make money. I did not have a permanent job to go to. I left my past behind, and my future was there for the taking. Hastily signing myself up with secretarial temping agencies, I started work as an office temp, completing various secretarial assignments in the City, often on a 1 week contract basis.

I then started looking for permanent work. I secured 4 interviews in 1 day. Upon completing the 4 interviews, I had 3 job offers on the table. I remember thinking that London was amazing! The salaries were double what I had previously been paid, and the companies who had offered me employment were very well respected law firms - I could take my pick. I chose the largest law firm which I had interviewed with, and asked them to increase their salary offer (I'm a firm believer in 'if you don't ask - you don't get'). When the increased salary request was considered, and a higher starting salary was counteroffered – I readily accepted. The law firm I commenced employment with, had a total of 600 employees in one building. Situated next to the river Thames, in a fabulous location in the City of London on London Bridge (I actually watched a James Bond speed boat chase being filmed for several days, from my office building). I was immensely proud to have secured the role of legal secretary, at a top London law firm, at the grand age of 20, and was 100% committed to my new employer.

However, the legal sector (which I stayed in for many years) is not for everyone. Back then there was a class divide between lawyers and secretaries which I was not familiar with, as having worked previously for a provincial firm was definitely less hierarchical. In London lawyers had status, power and enormous salaries – secretaries didn't. The class divide was very obvious, and on occasion I found it uncomfortable.

The law firm was like a machine, churning out contracts, leases and correspondence on a scale that I had never seen before. Secretaries literally plugged themselves in to their transcription headphones on arrival into the office, and there they remained for the majority of the day. The click clacking of keyboards was relentless. 80 wpm was considered to be slow. Case files and tapes would stack up on your desk, before your current cassette was finished. But it didn't bother me – because I was earning the money, and very good money.

My contact with clients was now next to zero, at times I felt I was in a factory, but the camaraderie amongst the legal secretaries was great. Our secretarial team were a very sociable bunch, and we were often found drinking pink champagne (which we paid for with our own salaries) in the lawyer's bars, on Thursday evenings. We rubbed shoulders with the city slickers and brokers on neutral ground, and it felt good.

Legal firms, in leading cities, will still pay top money for excellent legal secretaries and PAs, and it's worth considering law as a specialism. The office environment is impressive, the perks are good, you will be required to work hard, but if you're saving for a deposit on your first property – it could help you achieve it in a shorter time period, than in a different industry.

Finance (an industry I transferred into from law) is a similar professional, private sector, environment. Finance includes financial services companies, such as insurance and investment companies, accountancy firms, auditors and banks. These too carry the weighty salaried roles, but of course you will be expected to work hard for them. The top paid EA and PA positions in London are generally supporting senior executives in legal or financial services, property or investment companies, and can earn in excess of £60,000 (€79,000). These industries are very corporate, very professional and you will need to dress and act appropriately. EAs in finance, from my experience, have a very polished and professional approach, as they are representing key individuals in multi million pound businesses, and are also representing the brand itself.

If you choose to head into the financial services environment, you may work for a company with over 50,000 employees. Can you imagine that? The size of some organisations are vast. No doubt your office interior will be beautifully designed, the impressive building will be constructed of glass and stainless steel, and situated in the financial district of town.

Ultimately, the professional standing associated with working for a large financial services company – is extremely desirable. Having a 'Bank' on your CV is a bonus and will boost your pedigree. During my career, I've been fortunate enough to support Board level Directors at both the Halifax Bank of Scotland (HBOS) and The Bank of Ireland. So I have first-hand experience of working for a large, global, corporate, and those roles have ultimately paved the way for further successes during my career.

Choosing your career path

The higher you go up the corporate ladder – surprisingly – you have less direct contact with clients. You will become an 'internal' operator. You probably won't be close to the product or service which your company provides. You will become ensconced in the management structure of the organisation, the internal machine which drives the company, and that isn't for everyone. It can feel isolating.

If you really enjoy meeting people, providing a level of customer service and interacting with the public, you may be better suited to life in the public sector, or a smaller private company. Public sector industries include health, education, environment, transport, local or central government, social services, tourism, trade associations, and the justice system. As public sector organisations are funded by local or central governments, the salaries will invariably be lower. However, the PA roles found in the public sector may be more rewarding. You could be working in a more informal environment, and it may suit your personality. This could result in a less pressurised environment to work in, and therefore be less stressful.

Also worth considering, if you personality is big, and its creativity which you thrive on, are the industries of media, design, fashion, advertising or publishing. Perhaps you crave the more relaxed 'no suits' environment with bright offices and play areas, which can be found with tech giants such as Facebook, Google and Twitter.

Google Campus, Dublin.

Creative environments can also be found in architectural practices, PR, marketing and entertainment. If it's a fast paced and forever changing industry you are seeking, try outsourcing, retail or technology. Sometimes, your personality will dictate which environment is right for you. Whether you prefer structure, governance, a fixed hierarchy and a smart dress code, or you prefer open, modern offices, a casual dress code and a flatter structure – there is a company, within a sector, which will suit you. You just have to find it.

 Complete further research on the web into your chosen sector and industry. Consider temping in that environment so you can experience that sector first hand. Many companies provide temp to perm opportunities or short term contracts.

Currently, I'm employed in the outsourcing industry. Outsourcing involves the contracting out of a business process, or transferring the management of customer communications to another party. Basically, one company employs another, to run an area of its business, but it still operates under one company name and brand. Think call centres - customer service agents engaged in live chat, telephone reservation agents, customer service helplines, and online shopping. Companies also outsource back office processes such as human resources, facilities, marketing and research. Its big business, and very competitive. I thoroughly enjoy working in outsourcing as it's extremely fast paced, and very changeable. I enjoy the pressure and daily challenges, it keeps me focused and stimulated.

If temporary assignments are hard to find in your chosen sector or industry, and it's your experience you want to build upon, consider voluntary work. Approach local employers for any opportunities e.g. schools, estate agents, hotels. Any establishment that has an office or reception area can provide you with first-hand experience, to use in your employment search.

Interestingly, outsourcing is an industry which I hadn't considered, until a position came up with a company called Integreon, in their London office. It was my first experience in the outsourcing industry, and I thoroughly enjoyed it. Whilst at Integreon, I organised several high profile client events, including client dinners in the private dining rooms at The Gherkin, London and the Ardour Restaurant at the St Regis Hotel in New York. I also co-ordinated a management retreat, which involved 16 guests travelling to 2 stunning private villas in Provence, for a week's stay of strategy planning and team building.

Two years of supporting the EVP of business development at Integreon and my role, amongst several others, was unfortunately made redundant due to a massive company restructure. As luck would have it, within 2 weeks of my redundancy confirmation, the position of Executive Assistant to the CEO UK of Teleperformance was advertised. Teleperformance specialise in providing customer care solutions, and customer experience management, globally. The role itself was based in Bristol, the City in which I was living at that time.

It was an opportunity too good to miss. My 2 years of specific, outsourcing, industry experience was enough to secure me an interview, in addition to an already impressive CV. Those 2 years also stood me in good stead for the challenges I would face in my new role, and the terminology being used. It demonstrates that relevant industry, and sector experience matters. It will support you in your job application, and help you hit the ground running when you commence a new role, in a particularly specialised environment. This experience also demonstrated to me that if you are made redundant, potentially, a better job opportunity could be waiting for you, just around the corner!

Fortunately, I was successful in my application for the role of executive assistant to the CEO UK at Teleperformance. Four years down the line, I'm still enjoying my role, my responsibilities, and the daily challenges which come with supporting a CEO and Country Head, who is leading a UK company of 10,000 employees. I've reached a definite high point in my career, and I'm immensely proud to support board level directors who are industry leaders, and experts in their field.

Getting your foot on the ladder to C-Suite

If C-suite is your chosen destination (supporting the C-list executives e.g. CEO, CFO or COO) then you have ambition, and rightly so. Set you sights high and you will get there – eventually. A strong CV, and a solid work experience history, will help you. Employers will be looking for gaps in your work history, so avoid that, and also the length of time you have stayed with each employer. I believe that 2-3 years per employer is long enough to prove yourself, and either be promoted, to work for a more senior executive or, if the opportunities really aren't there, you should move on. Loyalty is sometimes unrewarding, so why wait if there is nothing to wait for. The average company CEO heads a company for approximately 5 years before moving on to their next project. If 5 years is long enough to turn a business around and enjoy its successes, then 2-3 years is long enough to establish yourself, get noticed, and move upwards.

Throughout my career, I have pro-actively pushed for the promotions or internal moves, but sometimes the opportunities just aren't there. If your company's hierarchy does not allow room for growth, or the existing PA to the CEO has maintained his or her role for the past 10 years, and has no desire to depart – then you've hit the ceiling. No matter how good you are at your job, you've reached a dead-end. So be pragmatic and plan your exit strategy. Remember, you can plan methodically as you're in full time employment, and can look around the job market at your own pace. Refresh your CV, update your LinkedIn profile, and ask for colleague endorsements. Upload any supporting information possible onto your LinkedIn profile. If you feel a certain MS Office skill is rusty, complete some free online training – or visit YouTube tutorials for advice. Brush up on your skills. Ensure that everything you present about yourself, prior to hitting the recruitment agencies, is up to date, professional, and the best it can be.

When you are ready to re-enter the world of recruitment – pick your employment agency wisely. Some will advise you that they have the best positions on their books, with the employers you are targeting – when they don't. Look online to see who is actually getting the best vacancies. Target the agencies, who have the top jobs. An agency who genuinely does have the top end jobs is Tiger Recruitment – so if you are looking for a new position in London or Dubai, it's worth contacting them. Get yourself back out in the market place, and when asked why you are looking to move, state with confidence that you are ambitious, and are seeking a vertical career move. Establish a good rapport with your chosen recruitment agency. It may be that the position you are seeking, isn't currently available, but if you have built strong relations with your agency contact, you can guess who he or she will call, when that dream job lands on their desk.

Spend time practising your interview techniques, and ensure your interview outfit is suitable for the sector and industry you have chosen. Furthermore, when you secure an interview, for that fabulous new role, complete your research on the company, and the executive who you will support. Expect a tough interview – and they get tougher depending on the level of the executive you will be supporting.

WE ARE MARKET LEADERS IN SOURCING TOP PA AND ADMINISTRATIVE STAFF AT ALL LEVELS.

Whether you are an experienced PA looking for an exciting new opportunity or a recent graduate looking for your first job in London or abroad, contact us today to secure the perfect role for you.

David Morel
CEO & Founder of Tiger Recruitment   **020 7917 1801**
David.Morel@tiger-recruitment.co.uk   **WWW.TIGER-RECRUITMENT.CO.UK**

In order to get to C-Suite, speak to your internal talent manager, regarding possible opportunities. Make it known that you are ambitions, and want to advance your career. Use your existing networking contacts for any external opportunities, and contact reputable recruitment agencies to register your interest for the top jobs.

Add to bible...

Add details of your chosen recruitment agencies, and your dedicated consultant, to your bible. Update this information with comments such as when you last spoke, the applications being processed etc. Use this as a point of reference to see which agency is being pro-active, and who you should phone to keep yourself top of mind.

When I secured my current position (supporting the CEO UK of Teleperformance) I had to complete 5 stages of interview, before I received the job offer. Yes really!! This consisted of a telephone interview, a face to face interview with an HR advisor, a skills test with a local recruitment agency, another HR face to face interview (but this time with the HR director), and the final stage was meeting my prospective boss! It did feel like an endurance test, however, I imagine those responsible for hiring the right person to support the CEO UK did not want to get it wrong, hence all the interview stages. Ultimately, if the jobs worth having – its worth fighting for!

4

Diary Management

What's in this chapter?

Diary Management is a one of a PAs strongest, and most frequently used skills. This underestimated **super skill** is what will set you apart from your peers, and get you noticed by your boss. Working away diligently in the background, moving meetings, advising of your executive's availability, agreeing meeting dates with external parties, and declining meetings on your executive's behalf, will consume your normal working day (if you are supporting a senior level executive). For those of you who are working your way up the career ladder, diary management will demand upwards of 40% of your time, every day. Which is why diary management is a skill every PA needs to master, and execute with military precision. In this chapter we will discover:

- The importance of diary management
- Tools for diary management
- Configuration of your executive's diary
  - Diary protocol and diary fact finding
- Outlook settings
  - Office hours
  - Holidays
  - Time zones
  - Delegate permissions
  - Diary privacy
  - Synchronisation
- Annual scheduling
  - Existing recurring meetings
  - Personal appointments
  - Upwards vertical meetings
  - Downwards vertical meetings

The importance of diary management

The diary, when managed correctly, is a well-oiled machine. It is 100% accurate, everything has been scheduled to deadline, with the correct attendees at the correct location, or by using the correct bridge number. Your diary management, if carried out effectively, brings order to your executive's chaotic working day, it provides structure to a pressurised environment, and it controls your executive's working hours, and eliminates the time stealers.

Professional diary management is a craft, and a lot of it comes with experience. But how do you gain the experience? Well, I've managed some pretty meaty diaries in my career, and I'm about to share my skills with you. My experience spans 22 years, I've managed diaries for global EVPs, global Board members, and global CEOs. I have diary managed for a financial services Board director – who was a member of 16 Boards (the total number of subsidiary companies operating under one parent company), and that was a challenge!

I am going to share with you the importance of diary management, how to configure your executive's diary, the significance of annual scheduling, how to improve your Outlook settings, and of course a few epic 'top tips' which will save you time, and increase your efficiency and productivity. Diary management is challenging, creative, a constant, and very rewarding. There is nothing more satisfying than managing an amazingly busy weekly schedule, involving flights, conference calls, meetings, transfers and client dinners, when at the end of the week you know your diary management has run to time, without issue and you've helped your executive enormously.

What is diary management? It's the term used to describe running your executive's office diary. Usually from 0900 Monday morning through to 1730 on Friday. Each day is split into hourly time slots, and the PA controls the contents of those slots. The working week will usually consist of diary entries for internal meetings, external meetings, conference calls, video conference or web hosted calls, site or client visits, travel, client entertainment, and allocated project time.

In addition to displaying the many meetings, and appointments, during the working week, the diary is also used for recording reminders, deadlines, private appointments, travel arrangements, hotel reservations and blocking dedicated time for research, analysis and review. Diary time can be scheduled for specific tasks, such as finalising the monthly sales report, reviewing the sales pipeline, or writing a presentation or speech. Entries in your executive's diary helps them to become more focused, deliver their reports on time, and work to deadline. It allows work prioritisation, and time to be allocated for time critical tasks. Non urgent items can also be regularly diarised so that they do not slip from the radar, for example: invoice approvals, travel approvals or expense reporting. These are tasks which can run the risk of being postponed, due to higher priorities, but need to be managed, and actioned, for internal reporting purposes.

Use the diary for scheduling time, for non-urgent tasks to be actioned by your executive e.g. invoice approvals and expense approvals. Schedule 1 hour a week so that these tasks are kept up to date.

The diary is the mechanics of your executive's working life. It is the hub of all of their activities. It is the tool you use, to manage your executive's time. It provides structure to their day, and improves their productivity by eliminating time stealers and other interruptions. In the public sector, diary management could be 100% of your role, if you are supporting a senior government official. In central government, the role is often split so a government minister has a dedicated 'diary manager', and the use of a separate PA for non diary tasks.

Managing your executive's diary is a massive undertaking, and not one to be taken lightly. It is your responsibility to ensure that the correct meetings appear in the diary, and that unnecessary demands upon your executive's time are either declined or delegated elsewhere. It is your responsibility to plan the navigation across the working week, and how your executive travels from A to B to C (and returns to A) in time for that 1600 meeting or call. It is your responsibility to avoid meeting clashes, double bookings and unnecessary travel, where a conference call could be scheduled instead. A good diary manager will instinctively know when a meeting can be declined, or postponed, or scheduled as a call, or as a face to face meeting.

Imagine what would happen without diary management? Your executive would have constant demands placed upon them, colleagues would be calling them at any time of the day, clients would be calling them without prior warning, and clients could turn up at your office without phoning ahead. It would be pure chaos. Nobody can work effectively in that environment. To plan ahead is to get ahead, and allows your executive to be organised, prepared, well informed and in control.

Diary management

To manage a diary successfully, you must have the ability to be organised, enjoy the attention to detail, and be a creative thinker. You also need to be incredibly flexible and versatile. More often than not, your beautifully crafted diary, all complete from Monday to Friday, will suddenly be pulled apart with an urgent client visit, or unexpected need to travel. You'll feel like you want to pull your hair out, as all your hard work is completely wasted, and you now have to start afresh. Not only do you have to make new arrangements, but you have to unpick your existing arrangements. This can be incredibly frustrating, however, this usually happens due to an unforeseen business requirement, and cannot be anticipated. You have to take a deep breath, think of it as a new challenge, and commence the re-working of the diary. I never complain or moan to my executives when this happens – it's nobody's fault, so just pick yourself up off the floor and get on with it. PAs are professional diary managers – so deal with it.

The diary is also your gatekeeping friend. It supports you, when unsolicited callers are requesting time with your executive. You can honestly explain to callers, that in order to speak with your executive, they would need to have a scheduled appointment, and therefore you cannot transfer their call. How does the caller make an appointment? They should put their request in writing and email it to you. Simple. The caller now understands that you operate an efficient appointment system, and they know what they need to do, to try and secure diary time.

This form of gatekeeping, also works with unwanted internal requests, e.g. 'Can I just pop in and see the CEO to discuss overheads please – it will only take 5 minutes?' Advise the requester that you need to check the diary, only to find that your executive is due to join a conference call in 2 minutes, and so you know he won't have time for this impromptu conversation. State that you can look for a free slot, and will put time in the diary when it's convenient for both parties.

Using the diary as gatekeeper, is something which you need to promote to others, so they understand there isn't a quick access route to your executive (unless it's something urgent). Respecting individuals scheduled time is important, and if you find some colleagues are not respecting this, then politely remind them that you manage the diary, and in order for it to run smoothly, they must look to you first, to secure time. Repeating this message, and re-enforcing it, will help you, to help your executive. Don't be shy about this – you're just doing your job.

The flipside of this, is when a colleague of yours has secured time in your executive's diary, they know that they will have completely dedicated, and focused, time with your executive, without interruption. That is worth a great deal, and you will be respected for facilitating that.

Use the diary as an additional 'gatekeeper' for your executive. Deter colleagues from contacting your executive without an appointment, and promote good practice by pre-booking diary time.

In my opinion, and with many years' experience in this field, the PA is the rightful manager of the diary. Some executives may be reluctant in the beginning to hand over the reins with complete autonomy but, with trust, that's what you want to achieve. You must become the 'go to' person for anything 'diary', and your executive must discourage individuals from approaching him/her direct. They should re-direct all enquiries to you, thus providing a consistent approach. You can discuss this with your executive, and suggest ways which you can manage more, on their behalf, if this isn't already happening.

Executives really need to hand over the diary management to the PA, as it sits within the PAs remit. PAs should be responding to meeting invites, checking diary availability, and responding to internal enquiries for free time. It is the PAs duty to manage this process, and thereby give time back to the executive, who no longer has to focus on such matters. PAs are professional diary managers, who can juggle appointments, deal with meeting clashes, and move things at short notice for an urgent request. Encourage your executive to let you take the strain.

So, we now know the importance of diary management, and how it effects the day to day life of our executive. Next, we will take a look at what tools are available for diary management.

Tools for diary management

Tools available to today's PA, in relation to diary management, are the best they have ever been. We have seen a radical development of tools, and devices, across the last 20 years which, thankfully, provide us with up-to-date, real-time, shared diaries, wherever your executive may physically be, and in whichever time zone. The advances are so fantastic, that I have the ability to schedule a new meeting in my manager's diary, only for him to read that entry within seconds, even if he is in another continent. Real-time diaries have enabled the PA, and business executive, to still have that close link, even when they are thousands of miles apart. In a way, it has brought the partnership closer together, with the executive more reliant on the PA, as the PA still retains control on all things 'diary' from base camp.

I had first-hand experience of diary management - before we had such great technology. Do you remember the Filofax? Or the desk diary which was a weighty A4 sized diary, with a hard bound cover? No? OK – that's just me then! We did the best we could, with the limited tools we had available. Ultimately, it meant that the executive still had to manage their own diary (whilst on the move), as it wasn't possible to have shared access to the physical diary. The executive would then update the PA, on return to the office, with any new appointments they had agreed whilst out. I think the technological developments have definitely assisted, and added, to the scope of the PA role. We now have far more control, and access to the diary, than we had over a decade ago.

I do remember that historically (pre Blackberry), many portable devices didn't seem to talk to each other, or even the main network, so your executive was probably looking at a different version of the diary, than the one at your disposal. Devices, such as Palm Pilots (or PDAs) were often 'backed up' when they were in the office, and manually attached to the PC or laptop to refresh. It was a bit of a technical minefield, with PDAs trying to replace manual diaries, and palm devices not being up to scratch, or losing data.

Thankfully, those days are in the past, and advances in technology have simplified the sharing of diaries. Today's software allows us to view synchronised diaries, across multiple devices.

Today, the PAs most commonly used piece of diary management software is 'Microsoft Outlook'. This is part of the 'Microsoft Office' suite and if you have this in the workplace, it's probably the full 'professional' version. Restricted versions are available to purchase for home use, which are less expensive. Microsoft Outlook 2016 is the latest version of Outlook. Previous versions include Outlook 2013, Outlook 2010, and Outlook 2007. Microsoft Outlook groups together several, related, tools in one application, including: email, calendar (or diary), task manager, contact manager, note taking, journal, and web browsing.

Microsoft Outlook is compatible with the majority of devices, allowing your executive to view the diary on whatever device they use. Most commonly, your executive will have a laptop for the company office or home office use, plus smaller, mobile, devices to use when in transit e.g. a tablet, notebook, or smartphone. Your IT support team will ensure that the diary you manage synchronises across all of your executive's devices. Microsoft Outlook will also synchronise across different mobile phone platforms (e.g. iPhone, Android, BlackBerry and Windows). So, it doesn't matter which device or brand your executive prefers. Synchronising Outlook across your executive's devices also enables them to access their contacts, and emails, in addition to their diary, wherever they are.

Add to bible... Ask your executive what devices they are running, note the
 make and model number and add to your bible. If there are any sync problems in future, you now have the device details to provide to Tech Support.

Believe it or not, there were rivals to Outlook, e.g. Lotus Notes (which I found particularly un-user friendly and clunky). However, Microsoft Office has gained the monopoly of business users, so Outlook tends to be the office standard for professional diary management. Having one piece of software dominate the market place, in this particular area, makes it easier to transfer your diary management skills from one employer to the next.

If Microsoft Outlook professional isn't something you are familiar with, you should definitely complete training to improve your skills. Training on such software doesn't have to involve enrolling on an online or classroom led course, which commands a considerable fee. There are loads of training resources and tutorials, available for FREE, online. Furthermore, if you are currently using an older version of Outlook in your workplace, and are considering a career move, now is the time to refresh your Outlook skills by using free online training resources.

Many employers test IT skills prior to making a job offer, and MS Outlook is usually a test option, so always keep your Outlook skills up to date. It's also helpful to list the versions of Outlook you are familiar with, and have completed training on, on any job application and your CV.

Use FREE online training resources to improve your Outlook skills. There is no need to enrol on expensive web based or classroom led courses, when so much is available for FREE on the internet!

Try these resources for **FREE** Outlook training:

www.support.office.com
Microsoft Office's own training centre, with free downloadable training guides, and free video training. Training is available for different versions of Outlook, and different skill levels.
www.gcflearnfree.org
The Goodwill Community Foundation (GCF®) provides free online training, and online tutorials, for Outlook users. Work through 6 separate Outlook topics.
www.alison.com
ALISON is a global social enterprise, dedicated to providing free certified education, and workplace training skills. Online you will find free Outlook training with video content.

If you are looking for a tutorial to cover a specific task or problem you have in Outlook, then try YouTube. YouTube also contains many more general outlook tutorials which are all FREE to use. Just search for 'outlook tutorial' and take your pick of FREE online training videos.

Configuration of your executive's diary

Before you can get started with the actual diary management, you need to consider the basic set up of your executive's diary. Configuration of your executive's diary, is key to establishing a well organised and well managed diary. Spending time on the initial set up is paramount, and will pay dividends throughout the calendar year. Configuring your executive's diary is a task which should ideally be completed at the very beginning of your working relationship.

Diary protocol and diary fact finding

Establishing the way in which the diary is managed between you, and your executive, is key. We previously touched on the ownership of the office diary – and this definitely should sit with the PA. Sometimes there can be hesitancy, or resistance, from the executive to hand over the diary reins to the PA – in which case it's up to you to make your case for full management.

Situations such as this arise when an executive is perhaps promoted, and has not had the support of a PA before. They have managed their diary themselves, and cannot bear the thought of relinquishing the responsibility of something so important to somebody else. Another reason for an executive to be super cautious, is having had a bad experience with your predecessor. Perhaps the previous incumbent was disorganised, forgetful and inefficient (heaven forbid!). Your boss is nervous about placing his or her trust in you, due to previous incidents. The third likely situation is that as you are new in your post, your executive thinks you should 'ease into the role' and therefore you shouldn't diary manage from the beginning. This is also to be avoided. PAs diary manage – period. You don't need time to settle in – you are a professional, and this is what you are employed to do.

If you are transitioning into a new PA role, complete some background research on your future exec. Are they new to the role, have they had PA support before, what personality type are they? Background information will help you to understand what hurdles you may have to overcome, and which approach to take when managing the diary.

If you experience any 'diary hesitancy' from your executive, or you have just moved roles, and are at the beginning of your executive/personal assistant partnership, I would strongly suggest you do the following. Schedule a meeting with your boss to allow dedicated, uninterrupted time for you to address the 'diary protocol' issue. The aim of the meeting is to establish any existing diary issues, and agree on how the diary is managed going forwards. Talk to your boss, ask him/her how the diary was previously managed, what worked, what didn't. What would your boss like to be improved upon in the current diary structure? This is where you take the pro-active role, and suggest solutions to existing problems. It will soon become apparent, through a natural dialogue, what the problems are, what hang-ups (if any) your executive has, and what hasn't been implemented in the past.

If your boss hasn't had PA support previously, now is the time to explain how you propose to manage the diary. Explain the benefits e.g. freeing up their time, minimising disruptions, being the gatekeeper, allowing more focused work time etc.

 Schedule a meeting with your executive to discuss diary management. Ask your executive to give feedback on any existing issues. Understand what is and isn't working currently, and suggest possible solutions. Consider this to be you diary 'fact finding' mission.

During the diary 'fact finding' meeting, you also need to agree on the process of responding to meeting invites. This is when your boss receives an invite and either declines, accepts or replies tentatively. This is something which your boss will also find difficult to hand over. Personally, I always do this for my executives as I believe it is a diary manager's responsibility. However, there are a few hurdles to overcome before you can do this accurately. In order to allay your boss's, fears you need to have dialogue around their meeting activity.

Ask your executive to explain to you which regular meetings he/she attends, that are issued by somebody else, and which projects are a current priority - keep a record of this in your bible. This will help you to understand the key meetings, and re-occurring meetings, which your exec is invited to, and your executive's priorities. Without knowing this, you cannot make an informed decision on which meeting invites to accept, or decline. If this appears overwhelming in a new position, you could always ask your executive for a steer on the correct way to respond, as and when you receive a meeting invite – never guess.

Add to bible...

Add the list of meetings which your exec is invited to, to your bible plus any current internal projects. Refer to this when you receive meeting invites for your exec.

Next, you must discuss the regular meetings which your executive initiates. These are the meetings where your executive is the Chair, and the meetings are issued from your executive's diary. These meetings are 'owned' by your executive. Your executive decides when they are required, and who attends.

Diary management

The table below, shows actual meetings I scheduled for my previous executive, John Croft, whilst employed by a medium sized, international, outsourcing company. You will see that the meetings were scheduled across different time zones, so I also added the time zone conversions to the table.

REGULAR MEETINGS for EVP Global Sales

SMT Water cooler **15 min daily meeting**	
When: Mon, Thurs, Fri at 1430 UK / 0830 CST / 2000 IST for 15 mins. **Who: John / Alan / Kurian / Maria / Andrew** **NB calls do not take place Wednesdays due to CMT or EMT tacticals.**	
SMT Weekly Tactical **1 hour weekly**	
When: Tuesdays @ 1400 UK / 0800 CDT / 1830 IST - 1 hour call **Who: John / Alan / Kurian / Maria / Andrew**	
1 to 1 with Alan **1 hour weekly**	
When: Thursdays @ 1530 UK / 0930 CDT. 60 min call.	
Sales activity, Pipeline and DSO with Alan **30 minutes weekly**	
When: Mondays @ 1630 UK / 1030 CDT. 30 min call.	
1 to 1 with Kurian **1 hour weekly**	
When: Thursdays @ 1000 UK / 1430 IST. 60 min call.	
Sales activity, Pipeline and DSO with Kurian **30 min call weekly**	
When: Tuesdays @ 0900 UK / 1330 IST. 30 min call.	
1 to 1 with Andrew **1 hour weekly**	
When: Wednesdays @ 0900 UK. 60 min call.	
Sales activity, Pipeline and DSO with Andrew **30 min weekly**	
When: Mondays @ 0930 UK. 30 min call.	
Bill Weekly HR catch up **1 hour weekly**	
Thursdays @ 1730 UK / 1230 EDT. 60 min call.	

What you want to achieve, is a similar table, listing all of your executive's meeting subjects, the frequency, duration, attendees required, and the format of the meeting e.g. conference call, face to face, online/virtual. These meetings will be added to the diary in due course, but for now, record all the information provided to you, by your executive, during your diary fact finding meeting.

 Create a 'regular meetings' table, for all meetings owned by your executive, and add the table to your bible. Record the meeting subject, frequency, duration, attendees and format.

During the diary fact finding meeting - keep things positive, and always provide solutions to any problems which your executive outlines. Do not criticise your predecessor, or someone else's diary errors. You are the one with the solutions – the diary professional. Remember, that this is the beginning of a new partnership with your executive. There is no need to dictate how you are going to 'take over' the diary, this is about building trust and their confidence in you.

Now you have completed your diary fact finding mission, and have established the diary protocol, you should be in receipt of the following information:

- Any known problems with the current diary
- The changes your exec would like implemented with the diary
- An agreement on any diary changes you have proposed
- The process for accepting and declining meeting invitations
- A bible list of meetings which your executive is invited to
- A bible list of current projects which your exec is involved in
- A bible table of meetings owned by your exec, including subject, frequency, duration, attendees, meeting format and any time zone conversions.

By completing the fact finding meeting, you will also demonstrate to your executive, your professionalism, your desire to improve upon the existing process, and your eagerness to make a difference in your new role. We will revisit the information we've gathered in the bible (in particular the table of your exec's regular meetings) later in this chapter. But right now, we need to review your Outlook settings.

Outlook settings

As you are now in receipt of the basic diary structure, and have agreed how to manage it with your executive – it's time to look at the diary set up in Outlook. The diary (or Calendar) tool in Outlook is where you will build your executive's weekly diary. We are going to look at the following settings, which need reviewing in the Outlook calendar:

- Office hours
- Holidays
- Time zones
- Delegate permissions
- Diary privacy
- Synchronisation

NB I am using Outlook Professional 2013, and refer to those settings during the configuration and set up.

Office hours

You know what your company's standard operating times are, so we will change the calendar to reflect this. In Outlook go to Calendar/File/Options and select calendar from the list on the left. In the work time section, amend the start and end times accordingly. I use 0800 to 1800 as I know my executive will participate in meetings during those times. Check the boxes for working days in the week. Select OK. These settings will now change your calendar view, so that the times and days selected, show as possible meeting slots. This is also used to show other users on your network, your executive's potential availability.

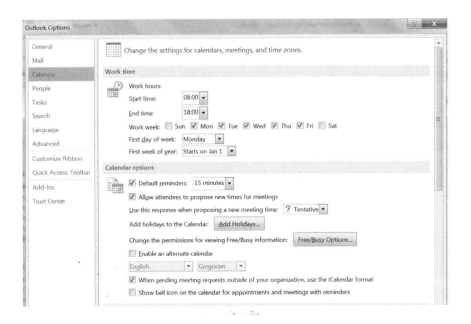

Holidays

Underneath work time options, in calendar options, you will see a button named 'add holidays'. This setting allows you to add public holidays to your diary. However, if you wish to add public holidays to your exec's diary, you will need to change the Outlook settings on your exec's laptop or desk top, (it is not possible to change your exec's holiday settings from your own Outlook folders). Select 'add holidays' and check the box next to the country you are located in. Then check the boxes of any additional countries, whose public holiday dates also need to be displayed. Select 'OK', Outlook will auto populate the diary with the public holidays you have chosen. This is actually very useful, if you are supporting an executive who regularly travels to another country. You may also wish to add the country where your company's HQ is based, or the country in which your executive's line manager is based. For example, your executive is based in the UK, his boss is based in the US, so you would add US holidays to

the diary, to prevent your exec contacting his or her line manager during a federal holiday. If your company's HQ is in Paris, then download France's holidays, so you understand when your company HQ is not operating. This also helps when you are scheduling meetings which involve your international colleagues, as you will automatically be aware of any public or national holidays.

No PA wants to issue an international conference call, to several participants, only to receive several replies stating 'this is a public holiday'.

If you work for a global organisation, research where your company's headquarters or registered office is. Add that country's public or federal holidays to your diary, and your boss's diary so you are aware when your colleagues are absent.

Time zones

In the same window you will also find time zone settings.

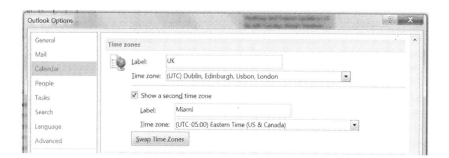

Ensure you select the correct time zone for the country in which you live, and label it. Outlook will automatically update the time zone for you, when your country's daylight saving time changes, so you don't need to manually change that. MS Outlook offers the function of showing a secondary time zone in the diary view. You may be doubtful as to why you would ever need this – but I use this all the time. It's particularly helpful if you are supporting a 'road warrior', a frequent business traveller who is often overseas, travelling across different states or continents. When you work with multiple locations across different time zones, it's often helpful to display two time zones concurrently, in your calendar. Outlook lets you show a side-by-side hourly scale beside the calendar, for easy reference.

The following screen shot shows the local time in Los Angeles and the secondary time zone in Canada (Newfoundland or Newfies for short).

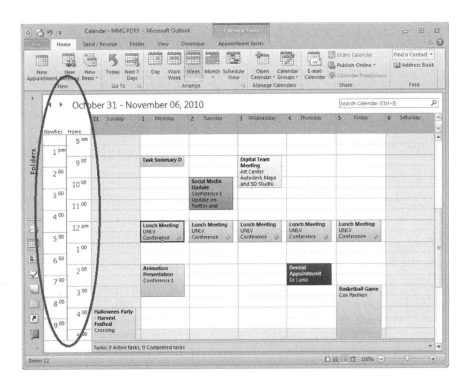

Diary management

Did you know that the United States has 9 standard time zones? If your boss is based in New York, and travelling to a meeting in Salt Lake City, they will cross into another time zone. New York is on Eastern time, whilst Salt Lake City observes Mountain time (2 hours difference). When you are working through the travel and diary arrangements for this trip, it is advantageous to have both time zones visible in your diary, so you can add the diary entries across the correct time zones. Having Outlook show two time zones at once, is simpler than having to calculate the difference, or to look it up every time you're considering the equivalent time at the second location.

Furthermore, if your boss is based in London and travelling to Manila, I would recommend showing the second time zone of Manila in the diary, whilst you are working on the trip co-ordination. An 8 hour time difference is huge. Being able to view both time zones, side by side, when co-ordinating the trip, scheduling appointments, and requesting meeting times with clients in Manila, will be a lot easier and reduces the risk of error.

Another benefit of displaying a secondary time zone in the calendar when your exec is overseas, is to flag the time difference for his or her meeting availability, with individuals in your local time zone. For example, should you be asked for your execs availability to join a BST time (London) conference call whilst they are on JST (Tokyo) time, you will see the limited window of corresponding times in an instant.

Moreover, showing your boss's local time in your calendar view, allows you to understand at a glance, what time of day your boss is experiencing, before you pick up the phone to him/her. It would be massively embarrassing for you to call your boss with an enquiry, only to realise that you've just called at 0300 and your boss was asleep! Having said that – my executive has actually called me at 0200, forgetting the time zone difference, on that trip!

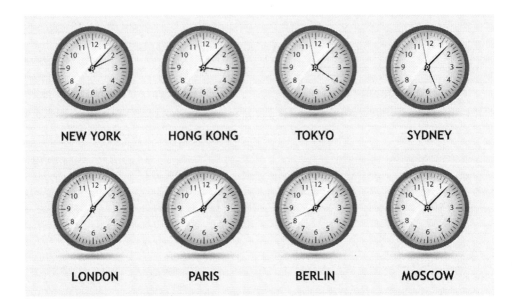

NEW YORK   HONG KONG   TOKYO   SYDNEY

LONDON   PARIS   BERLIN   MOSCOW

If you are not familiar with the Outlook secondary time zone view, try it. The next time you are co-ordinating international or interstate travel for your executive – you'll find it a huge benefit.

Delegate permissions

These allow an executive to delegate certain permissions and responsibilities (within Outlook), to their PA e.g. viewing and amending the calendar, issuing new meeting requests direct from their calendar, and responding to meeting invitations on their behalf. Changing the settings will also create rules, so that meeting requests automatically appear in the PAs (delegate's) inbox (in addition to the executive's email account) so that you can manage the diary from your own diary view. These settings can be found in File/Account Settings/Delegate Access.

You can amend your own delegate settings via your laptop or PC, but to change your executive's delegate settings, you will need to either ask them to make the amends themselves, or action on their behalf, using their PC or laptop (you cannot change their settings from your device).

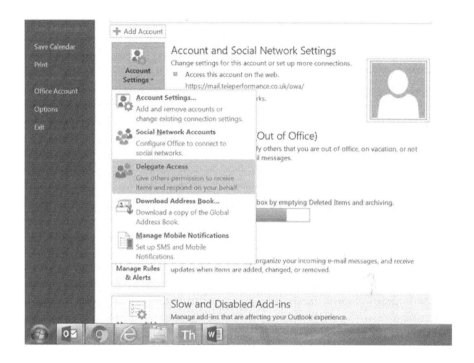

Firstly, the executive needs to determine the level of access that their PA is granted to their Outlook folders. They can award various levels of delegate permissions, depending on how much responsibility they want to handover, and how much access. By default, when you add a delegate, the delegate has full access to the Calendar and Tasks folders only – not email. The different levels of delegate permissions are:

Reviewer: the delegate can read items in the executive's folder.
Author: the delegate can read and create items, and change and delete items that he or she creates. For example, a delegate can create task requests, and meeting requests, directly in their Task or Calendar folder, and then send the item on the executive's behalf.
Editor: the delegate can do everything that an Author has permission to do, and additionally, can change and delete the items that an executive created.

Secondly, we will make the necessary changes to Outlook to implement the transfer of responsibilities of diary management to you. To change your executive's delegate permissions, first agree a time with your executive to complete this exercise, when they are next in the office. Select 'delegate access' via your executive's Outlook, and select your name from the 'add' button. The delegate permissions will appear showing the default settings – which will award you editor rights to the calendar only (see next screen shot). Ensure that the check box 'delegate receives copies of meeting related messages' is ticked, so that you receive your execs meeting invites, and can accept and decline, direct from your inbox. Your exec will receive a duplicate invite, but will see the action you have taken from their view.

To grant delegate access to the email inbox and contacts, you will need to amend the permissions by selecting the drop down arrows for those functions, and selecting either Reviewer, Author, or Editor. Remember 'Editor' has full rights. If your executive wishes to keep his/her email inbox private, then change the Calendar settings only. Select OK, and test your access by creating a test meeting appointment in your executive's diary, from your diary view.

It's entirely your executive's decision which of these delegate permissions they grant you. At the very least – you will need full **calendar editor** rights, to enable you to manage their diary effectively.

Diary privacy

Whilst you are completing this exercise, it's also advantageous to check out who is already listed as having delegate permissions to your executive's diary. This is probably a setting, your exec hasn't accessed for a considerable time, and more than likely is not aware of who can, or cannot, see their folders. Personally, I err on the side of caution when awarding others with read (reviewer) rights to my executive's diary. I always flag to an executive, once I have started in a role, who already has existing read or editor rights to their diary / their email and their contacts. Sometimes the results are surprising, and more often than not, your executive has no idea why there are 6-10 people who are showing as reviewers of their diary. That's potentially 6-10 colleagues who are viewing your executive's diary - without your executive's express permission.

Review who has delegate access to your boss's diary by checking the delegate permissions. Ask your boss to confirm who needs access and who can be removed.

Once you've checked this with your executive, you need to go through the delegate access permissions together with your exec, and decide who actually needs it, and who doesn't. If you cannot check these permissions on your exec's own device (as they are travelling or away from the office for a long period of time), you can ask your IT department to check these settings for you. When you have agreed who requires delegate permissions, remove those colleagues who no longer need access.

Furthermore, explain your rationale for completing this exercise, and remind your boss that any diary enquiries should be addressed to you in future as 'diary manager'. Individuals should not make their own assumptions of your executive's availability, by dipping in and out of his/her diary directly.

Restricting viewing rights reinforces that process, and helps to improve the confidentiality and integrity of your boss's diary. Why would your colleagues need access to your exec's diary directly? As the PA, you are now the diary manager so for the sake of consistency, remove others, so that colleagues approach you directly for a decision or availability.

Protecting your boss's diary from unsolicited viewing, is also important for business reasons. For example, your boss is working on a restructure of the operational team, and there are various meetings scheduled with the HR director, on this topic, regarding redundancies. If this information was viewable by unauthorised individuals, it could be damaging within the company, before any kind of internal announcement is made. Likewise, with regards to employment interviews, details must be kept confidential, particularly at a senior level. Candidates' names should be especially protected who are interviewing from external, competitor, companies. Protecting the diary itself, is a sure way of doing this.

Reducing visibility of your boss's diary, to a limited number of colleagues, is definitely best practice. Anyone internal will still be able to view blocks of 'free time and busy time', and ultimately they should be approaching you as 'keeper of the diary' for any diary enquiries.

It's important to keep your exec's diary private from public view. Sharing too much information could be detrimental in the company, and confidential information could be leaked by sharing the calendar with others. Minimise the risk and keep it private.

Synchronisation

An important part of the configuration process, is the synchronisation of the diary, email and contacts, across all of your executive's devices. Otherwise known as 'syncing', this is slightly more technical, and definitely requires the use of your tech team support. Today's business executives are mobile individuals, often frequent travellers, and are expected to be able to conduct business wherever they are. Mobile executives demand the latest technologies to keep them connected, and in constant contact with their email, contacts and folders, whenever and wherever, they need them.

Your executive is no doubt running multiple devices, whilst on the move. Commonly, the laptop is used when in the office or at home, a tablet or notebook when travelling, and a smartphone when time is limited, or for quick responses. Therefore, your executive relies upon each device to hold the most up-to-date, and accurate information, for their means of reference and communication.

Each device must therefore replicate the main Outlook folders e.g. diary, email and contacts. The latest information needs to be at the fingertips of your executive – no matter which device they are using or travelling with. With today's technology this is possible, but it does take an IT professional to complete the set up (and test), before you can be confident that this works 100%.

Previously, you've already recorded all the devices, makes and model numbers that your executive is operating. Raise a ticket with your IT support desk for them to sync the Outlook calendar, contacts and email across all devices, and complete testing to ensure this has been successful. You will need to liaise with the IT support desk on your exec's whereabouts, and book a date when your exec can bring all of his/her devices into the office, for IT to work on.

Also worth bearing in mind, is that when your exec changes their main Microsoft Exchange password – it is likely that they will have to replicate this across all devices, otherwise they will experience sync issues.

 Periodically, ask your exec if everything is syncing properly across all of their devices. If not, manage the resolution process, and liaise with IT tech support on your exec's behalf. It's important to iron out any glitches with synchronisation, as successful diary management only works - if the technology works.

Annual scheduling

We've added public/federal holidays into the calendar using Outlook, however, there are many more entries to consider when configuring your exec's diary. The initial calendar set up will include adding holidays, private appointments, reminders, deadlines, family birthdays, annual events e.g. anniversaries, plus the recurring company meetings. Does you exec have children? If so, it's useful to add school term dates to the calendar. This information may or may not already be plugged into the diary by your predecessor – but don't assume this is accurate, check it. Treat the configuration process as a clean slate. This is now your diary to manage, so you must start at the beginning and check the accuracy, and relevancy of existing appointments, before adding new ones.

In order to configure your exec's calendar for the year ahead, I think it's easier to break annual scheduling down into 4 sub sets:

- o   Existing recurring meetings
- o   Personal appointments
- o   Upwards vertical meetings
- o   Downwards vertical meetings

Diary management

Let's look at these subsets in more detail, to better understand the different components of your executive's diary.

Existing recurring meetings

If you have just taken responsibility for an existing diary, you can search for the recurring meetings which are already in place. This is also good preparation for your diary fact finding meeting, as you can share the search results with your exec, and go through the entries 1 by 1 for accuracy.

In the Calendar view, open your exec's calendar. Put the cursor in the searching box above the calendar, to activate the Search Tools in the ribbon. Select 'Search' from the top of your screen, select 'more' and 'recurring'. Select 'yes' from the drop down box. The search results will appear, showing you the recurring meetings which are in your exec's diary. View the 'end date' as some of these entries will have expired. It's the current entries you are interested in. View the 'recurrence pattern' column – this tells you the frequency of the meeting, time, date and duration.

If you are completing this search, post the diary 'fact finding' meeting with your boss, that's fine. Your boss has already confirmed to you which meetings are current (recurring), meetings, so you just need to cross check that information, with the search results. Remove any recurring meetings which are no longer required. Some recurring meetings, from the previous year, may not be relevant in the current year. This could be due to the end of a project, a sales pitch has since completed, or that new business win has moved across to the operations department. Furthermore, your exec may have attended a weekly strategy meeting, and that responsibility has transferred to another manager – again this is no longer current and should be deleted from the diary view.

 Run a search for all 'recurring' meetings in your exec's diary. Remove the recurring meetings which are no longer required from the diary, to keep the diary accurate and relevant.

Keeping the diary up to date, and accurate, is also about being pro-active. Your exec does not have the time to notify you that a series of meetings are no longer applicable, and can be deleted or declined. It's your responsibility to be on top of such things, which is why reviewing recurring appointments annually, or when you commence initial configuration of the diary, is vital. I like to complete this exercise in December, so that the diary is current and refreshed, before moving into the next calendar year. It also frees up additional time slots for new projects or meetings.

Personal appointments
Whilst the diary will hold predominately business meeting appointments and reminders, your exec does have a private life, so the business diary can be used to record important private appointments. As a PA, you will be privy to this information, which of course is to be treated in the strictest confidence. It is perfectly normal for your exec to add a medical or dental appointment in their diary, so that you can arrange the usual business appointments around it. Such entries can be marked as 'private' using the padlock icon, when you or your exec create a new diary entry, if necessary. This prevents others (with shared diary access) from reading the personal diary entry.

School holidays are also a necessary inclusion, if your exec has children of school age. School term dates vary by location, so make sure you have the correct information. Ask your exec to provide you with the school term dates (a link to the school website should suffice), and plug these details into the diary. I add these dates as 'all day events' showing as free time, so that the entry is visible at the top of the diary, and does not show as busy or blocked time. Adding term dates is also relevant, as it shows your exec when the national school holidays are e.g. easter holidays, summer holidays etc. These are periods when a vast majority of business people book their annual vacation, to correspond with their children's holidays. Even if your exec does not have children, colleagues and clients will do, so adding those key dates will be useful to know. It will help flag when people are likely to be taking annual leave, and therefore unavailable for discussions, meetings or decisions.

Rutland Term Dates 2015/2016

Term 1
Schools open Thursday 27 August 2015
Schools close Friday 16 October 2015
Term 2
Schools open Monday 2 November 2015
Schools close Friday 18 December 2015
Term 3
Schools open Tuesday 5 January 2016
Schools close Friday 12 February 2016
Term 4
Schools open Monday 22 February 2016
Schools close Thursday 24 March 2016
Term 5
Schools open Monday 11 April 2016
Schools close Friday 27 May 2016
Term 6
Schools open Monday 6 June 2016
Schools close Tuesday 19 July 2016

Other personal entries, to add to the diary, will include family member's birthdays, anniversaries and personal holiday dates. Prompt your exec for this information, and add to the calendar.

Add school term dates to your exec's diary. Even if your exec does not have children, they will know when colleagues, and clients (with children) are likely to be on holiday, and therefore not available for meetings.

Upwards vertical meetings

If you are employed by a large corporate, or a multinational organisation, your exec's diary will be vertically driven. This means that your executive's own diary appointments, will be structured around the meetings issued by the company's internal leadership team, or its executive board.

For example, starting with the very top tier of a global organisation, the global CEO or Chairperson's office will issue an 'annual meeting schedule' towards the end of the calendar year. This master document will detail all the senior executive meetings at the highest level, in your organisation, throughout the forthcoming year. The master document will be distributed to those required to attend the meetings, and their PAs only. Sometimes the CEO's office will back this up with Outlook meeting invites, sometimes not. It depends on the size of the organisation. If it's global, the likelihood is that only the document will be circulated, and it's down to individuals to enter the relevant meetings into their schedules. This is because large multinationals often operate across multiple servers and exchanges, so it's not always possible to locate colleague's email addresses on Outlook.

The 'annual meeting schedule' document is like a company bible (see example over), it will act as the back bone for all management activity. The schedule is to be treated with respect, as it no doubt took great pains for a Senior EA to produce. Due to the importance of the meetings, and the seniority of attendees involved, these meeting dates seldom move, once they have been communicated. The dates are 'set in stone'. This allows attendees to pre-plan and book any travel, or accommodation, well in advance, thereby obtaining the better rates and reducing travel costs. The following page contains an example 'annual meeting schedule' detailing the venue (Country), date, name of meeting, start time and time zone.

The Annual Meeting Schedule

Venue	Meeting Date	Meeting Name	Start time/zone
January			
Miami	Friday, January 11th	Executive Overview Call (EOC)	9:00am (Miami time)
Miami	Friday, January 25th	EOC	9:00am (Miami time)
February			
	Friday, February 8th	TPDS + TLS + GN	
	Monday, February 11th	Iberico – LatAm Board Meetings	
	Wednesday, February 13th	CEMEA Board Meetings	
	Friday, February 15th	Strategic Meeting	Morning
Paris	Wednesday, February 27th	Group Board Meeting	Starting at 3:00pm
Paris	Thursday, February 28th	Investor Conference	Morning until 1:00pm
March			
Miami	Friday, March 15th	EOC	9:00am (Miami time)
April			
Miami	Friday, April 26th	EOC	9:00am (Miami time)
May			
Miami	Friday, May 10th	TPDS + TLS + GN	
Miami	Monday, May 13th	Iberico – LatAm Board Meetings	
Miami	May 16th	CEMEA Board Meetings	
Paris	May 29th	Group Board Meeting	9:00am
Paris	Friday, May 31st	AGM	9:00am
June			
	Friday, June 7th	EOC	9:00am (Miami time)
July			

	Thursday, July 11th	EOC	10:00am (Miami time)
Paris	Tuesday, July 30th	Group Board Meeting	9:00am
	August		
	August 24th	EOC	9:00am (Miami time)
	September		
Miami	September 12th	TPDS + TLS + GN	
Miami	Monday, September 16th	Iberico – LatAm Board Meetings	
Miami	Wednesday, September 18th	CEMEA Board Meetings	
Miami	Friday, September 20th	Strategic Meeting	Until 1:00pm
	October		
	Thursday, October 10th	Benchmark and Budget Delivery	
	November		
Miami	Friday, November 8th	TPRS + TVS + GM	
Miami	Monday, November 11th	Iberico – LatAm Board Meetings	
Miami	Wednesday, November 13th	CEMEA Board Meetings	
Paris	Thursday, November 28th	Group Board Meeting	
	December		
	Friday, December 13th	EOC	9:00am (Miami time)

Let's imagine that your exec is a C-level director. They've just received the annual meeting schedule from the Group CEO's office, and have forwarded it to you, to manage. View the document, and highlight all the meetings your exec is required to attend. If that isn't obvious from the document itself, make time to go through this with your manager. Then, manually enter the relevant meetings into your executive's diary. Make a record of those specific meetings in your bible, together with a note to say that they have been diarised.

The annual meeting schedule will also list regional board dates, or group board dates, which your exec perhaps doesn't attend, but does submit a report to. You should add those dates into the diary - as a reminder for you and your boss. If the annual meeting schedule document has not been forthcoming, approach the Chairman's or CEO's office and request it. It's very important that you obtain this, as this builds the structure for your exec's diary.

The practice of issuing an 'annual meeting schedule' in large corporations is commonplace. Due to a global organisation's hierarchy, it is prudent to wait to receive the annual meeting schedule, before you, in turn, issue meetings on your exec's behalf. Meetings which are driven by executives, senior to your own manager, may be referred to as the 'upwards vertical'. Meetings which your exec issues downwards to his/her direct reports may be referred to as 'downwards vertical' meetings. An important fact I have learnt, is that it's imperative you wait for the upwards vertical, executive meetings, to be announced, before you start working on your bosses downwards vertical meetings. This is standard diary etiquette – ignore this at your peril. If you choose not to observe the diary 'etiquette', and issue your exec's meetings without waiting, you will have problems.

If you do proceed to schedule your bosses' diary, without knowing the executive meeting dates to avoid, you may be in conflict when those dates are issued. If that is the case, you will have to reschedule your meetings and apologise to the individuals involved. Save yourself the bother and wait. If you are being pressurised from subordinates or PAs in the business, regarding your bosses annual dates – ask them to be patient, and advise them you are waiting on the CEO's office, for company-wide dates, before you can proceed.

Add to bible... Add all meetings (upwards verticals), which your exec attends, into the diary and copy and paste the details into your bible for future reference. If information is missing e.g. the video conference number, a conference bridge or the meeting duration – enter a reminder in your diary to chase that information down, closer to the meeting date.

You now have the upwards vertical meetings confirmed and in the diary. Whatever meetings you issue from hereon in – you are safe in the knowledge that you will not clash with the annual vertical meeting schedule. The executive meeting dates have been communicated, and you can now proceed and publish your exec's diary dates, downwards, to your executive's team.

Downwards vertical meetings

Previously, you completed a diary 'fact finding' meeting with your exec, which established all the meetings your exec requires, during the calendar year. Refer to the 'regular meetings for EVP Global Sales' table earlier in this chapter. Obviously, there will be additional meeting requirements as the year progresses, but for now, you should understand the basic structure of meetings required on a weekly and monthly basis. Depending upon the seniority of your exec, and the nature of the business you are in, these will consist of a mixture of regular client meetings, board meetings, quarterly review meetings, and monthly reporting meetings.

Diary management

With regards to your exec's line management responsibilities there will be 1 to 1s to arrange, annual objective setting, 6 monthly progress reviews and weekly team calls. If your exec has budgetary control responsibilities, there will be additional finance meetings which need recording in the diary. These dates may be issued from your finance department, rather than your own exec, and will consist of regular deadlines for month end reporting, quarterly reporting, and quarterly budget v forecast meetings.

Furthermore, ensure that you have obtained information regarding any additional diary dates which are useful to your exec e.g. dates when internal auditors are on site, dates of annual trade exhibitions or conferences (which your exec would like to attend), plus your company's client entertainment activities such as the annual Celtic Manor golf tournament or the Cheltenham Gold Cup Festival.

 Ask your marketing department for the key dates in the company's marketing calendar, which impact upon your exec e.g. client entertainment events, trade shows, industry conferences and awards dinners etc. Add these events to the diary.

Diarise allocated time, to complete your downwards meeting scheduling. Treat this as a standalone project. Once you start this task, it's important to see it through to completion as quickly as possible - as other PAs in the business are waiting upon your diary invitations, before they issue theirs. The whole process is a diary cascade, and has a knock on effect to the subsequent tiers of your business.

Refer to your bible, and review the table of meetings owned by your executive. Firstly, we will prioritise which downwards meetings to issue, by order of importance. When I complete this annual exercise, I prioritise by focusing on the senior level meetings first (with the most senior attendees), and work my way down to the lower level meetings. Senior level meetings are meetings which include heads of department, senior managers, and your executive's peers. It's important to secure the time of those individuals which you know are very much in demand, before their diaries become too busy.

Once those meetings are scheduled, and you have secured time in the diaries with the most senior of your meeting attendees, it's time to focus on the larger/group meetings which your manager chairs (this is the second category of meetings which I prioritise). The more individuals required for a meeting, the longer it takes to co-ordinate. For example, for meetings with multiple attendees you are likely to be working with a different meeting format e.g. a conference call, video conference or online meeting, or scheduling the meeting across multiple time zones. Such meetings are more time consuming to arrange due to checking attendee availability, factoring in the meeting format, and booking the necessary meeting tools to facilitate the meeting connection.

The third and final category of meetings to schedule, from your execs table of meetings, are the more informal but regular catch ups. These are the 1 to 1s, the updates with team leaders and your exec's direct reports. This third group of meetings usually consist of 2 attendees, are often 30 mins to 1 hour max, and are pretty easy to secure in the diary – hence leaving those to last.

So we now know which downwards meetings to schedule first (senior level attendees), second (multiple attendee meetings) and third (informal and catch ups). In the next chapter we will learn how to issue the meeting invite, from the Outlook calendar.

5

How to schedule a meeting

What's in this chapter?

Coordinating a business meeting sounds relatively straightforward, but a professional PA will take into consideration many factors, before issuing a calendar invite. The invitation issued from your manger's Outlook diary, should be as professional as possible, contain all the relevant data, and provide the attendees with the resources they need to join the meeting. In this chapter we will review the key elements of meeting coordination, the resources required, how to send a calendar invite, how to find the perfect venue and understand some of the weird and wonderful phrases used in business meeting coordination. Subheadings include:

- Meeting requirements
- Attendee availability
- Meeting resources
- Additional meeting information
- Issuing the invite
- Scheduling etiquette
- Venue finding
- Meeting terminology

Invest time in your meeting co-ordination (before you issue the invite), and you will get this right first time. Accurate and comprehensive meeting invites are what you want to achieve, and what your exec expects. Remember that the invite, when issued, will appear to have been sent directly from your exec's Outlook folder, so it's imperative to be 100% accurate in your work. Let's look at the different elements of scheduling a meeting, in more detail.

Meeting requirements

As we've discovered in chapter 4, an Outlook calendar entry can consist of personal appointments, birthdays and anniversaries, project deadlines, reporting deadlines, board meetings, 1 2 1s, weekly team calls, client meetings and offsite supplier meetings - amongst other things. An Outlook **meeting** is when 2 or more people meet, and for the purpose of the PA, when you invite people to attend a meeting - with your executive. Meeting invites can be issued for meetings 'in person' e.g. a face to face meeting, or meetings when attendees cannot be present at the same location e.g. a conference call or online web conference.

Before you issue the diary invite from the calendar, there are a few things to consider. These include the meeting requirements, attendee availability, meeting resources, the information to include in the body of the invite, scheduling etiquette and meeting terminology. So, it's not as straightforward as originally anticipated, but that's why this is a skill. Hastily issuing a meeting invite, without giving it due consideration, will lead to error. Details will be

omitted, resources forgotten and this will end with confusion, and downtime
for those involved. All the information should be present, it shouldn't leave the
attendees asking you for further details about the location, dial in number or
subject matter.

Whether you are working though the annual schedule, and issuing recurring
meeting invites for your boss, or your boss has asked you to set up a brand new
meeting – the process for scheduling a meeting invite is basically the same.
Firstly, you need to understand the requirements of the meeting, by obtaining
the key information, which will be used in the 'new appointment' fields below.
The requirements are the bare facts of the meeting – who is involved, the
subject and the location.

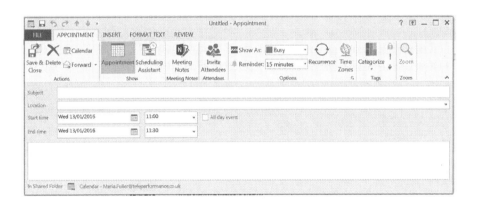

The appointment window will prompt for the following field entries: Subject,
Location, Start Date and Time, End Date and Time. Refer to the table below,
and obtain the relevant information from your exec.

Subject	To be typed in the subject line of the meeting invitation, confirming the topic of the meeting.
Location	Is this a face to face meeting, conference call or an online meeting? The exact location should be communicated e.g. meeting room name or location address, conference bridge number or online meeting details.

How to schedule a meeting

When	How soon is the meeting required (tomorrow, next week?). This helps when checking diary availability.
Duration	For what period of time is the meeting required
Recurrence	Is this a recurring meeting or a one off
Attendees	Who is required to attend the meeting

Let's imagine you've spoken to your exec and you've obtained the relevant meeting data. Your meeting requirements look like this:

Subject	Team Project Meeting
Location	Face to face at the Canary Wharf, London office
When	Within the next fortnight
Duration	1 hour
Recurrence	One off
Attendees	Your exec, Joseph Evans (external consultant), Jose Moreira, Carlo Cuttitta, Tiesha Britton and Robert De Boer.

So this is the 'Team Project Meeting' which your executive needs scheduling. Next we must check everyone's availability for this meeting, within the required timeframe.

Attendee availability

Before you select a time and date and issue the meeting invitation, the general rule is that you must check availability with the attendees required. Checking their 'availability' means checking for an available time in their diary, when they can attend the meeting. The one exception to this rule, is that I do not check availability when issuing my downwards meeting schedule, because having observed the hierarchy of annual meeting scheduling – this is not necessary. However, for all additional meetings, which do not form part of the annual scheduling, I strongly recommend you do check attendee availability. The attendees may already have existing diary commitments or be out of the office, or travelling.

It's advisable to check attendee availability, prior to issuing a meeting invitation. Attendees may already have existing diary commitments, be out of the office, or travelling.

MS Outlook has a tool for checking attendee availability, this is called the 'scheduling assistant'. You basically enter all the information into the 'new appointment' window, add the attendees required by selecting 'invite attendees', and select the attendees from the 'To' box. Select 'scheduling assistant', which will display blocks of free and busy times for all attendees. This provides you with an easy view of the common 'free' time, which you can select for your proposed meeting time, before you hit 'send'.

The problem with the 'scheduling assistant' is that it only works, if everyone is on the same Microsoft Exchange. For example, if the meeting requires internal colleagues only, and your company is relatively small and using one Microsoft Exchange, you can probably view all of the free and busy times via the scheduling assistant tool. However, if your company is across multiple locations, or in different countries, or you are inviting external contacts to the meeting, you will not be able to view their 'free or busy times' because that information is not available, as it's held on different servers.

Look at the 'Team Project' meeting snapshot, as an example. Joseph Evans is an external consultant, and is therefore not on your company's exchange. You have added him as an attendee and have selected 'scheduling assistant' to view free and busy times. Joseph has diagonal grey lines through his time slots, and if you were to hover your mouse over that Outlook would advise, in a pop up window, 'no information, recipient's server could not be identified'. Outlook has identified that Joseph is not on your company exchange, and so you have no way of knowing Joseph's availability, without asking him directly, or his PA (if he has PA support).

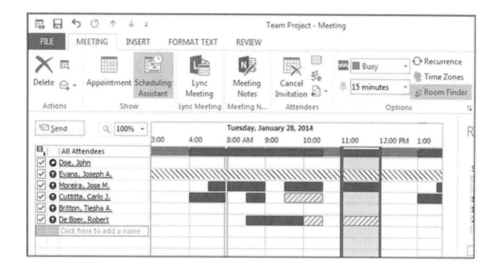

Similarly, if one of the attendees is an internal colleague, but happens to be based in the USA and you are based in the UK, their free and busy times will also not be viewable, due to multiple servers. So whilst 'scheduling assistant' is available as a tool for checking availability – it doesn't always work and can't be relied upon.

Scheduling assistant is also reliant upon the diary owner updating their diary regularly. If, for example, one of your attendees is showing as 'free' but in reality they have a private appointment, and haven't entered it on Outlook, you will have a problem. However, if scheduling assistant is successful and returns accurate free and busy times for all of your attendees, you can proceed and issue the meeting invite. Personally, my advice is not to do that. Sending an invite direct to attendees, without a personal communication via email beforehand, is slightly dictatorial and impolite. You haven't corresponded with the individuals concerned, or shown the courtesy of engaging with them to highlight this meeting requirement – or asked them if they are available. In my experience, it's always polite to ask attendees of their availability, via email, prior to issuing the calendar invite. Using the 'Team Project Meeting' as an example, this is how to correctly check attendee availability, and to determine the suitable date and time for your meeting.

Step 1: Propose meeting dates

View your exec's diary and select 3 potential dates and times for this meeting. Ensure they are across 3 different dates (to provide better flexibility to attendees). Issue the email below to the required attendees, from your mailbox, as follows:

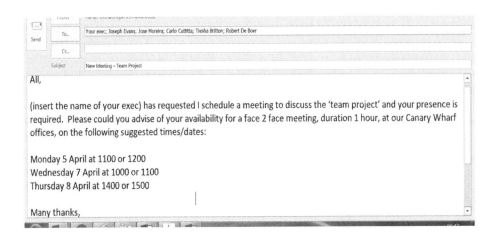

This email communication has achieved 3 things:

1. It has communicated the request for a new meeting;
2. It has shown courtesy in asking for individual's availability;
3. It has suggested 3 potential dates and times for this meeting.

Offering 3 meeting dates gives your attendees a certain degree of flexibility, in that they can advise of the most suitable date for their attendance. Imagine that not everyone is based at the Canary Wharf location, travelling to the meeting involves travel time, so offering 3 dates allows attendees to work through their travel options (dependent upon where they are based) and revert with the date, which suits them. Some attendees may also be busy on certain dates, and have their own meetings to attend.

The 3 Date Rule: always offer 3 dates when checking attendee availability. Offer more, and it requires too much time for attendees to check their diary and respond, offer less and you may not find a match. 3 is generally sufficient to find a corresponding date.

Step 2: Record the email responses received from the attendees

As you have emailed suggested dates to the attendees, the responses will also be received by email. This creates a record of the answers, easily viewable in your inbox folder. In order to collate the responses, I draw a simple grid, see example below, and I populate it with the responses, when received.

	5|4	7|4	8|4
JD	X	X	1400 or 1500
JE	✓	✓	✓
JM	X	1100	1400
CC	1100	1000	✓
TB	✓	X	✓
RB	1100	1000	1400

To use this method, draw a grid, and in the left hand column, add the initials of the delegates you have invited. In the header row, across the page, enter the dates offered. Populate the grid with a cross for 'not available', a tick for 'available' and if they can only do one time, add that specific time. Using this technique serves two-fold. One, you will see at a glance whether you have received all the responses, or not. And two, you will recognise which meeting date and time is the most convenient for everyone.

Step 3: Review the results of your attendee's availability, to find a mutually convenient meeting date and time

When the responses are received, you should go with the majority's preferred date and time. View the date columns vertically, to find your match. The answers shown in the example grid indicate that the 8 April at 1400 is convenient for everyone, and this is the time we will schedule.

Meeting resources

This is a factor which you must consider, and determine what's required. Meeting resources are the additional items you will need, to facilitate the meeting e.g. a meeting room, flip chart, projector, display screen, any connection cabling, additional power points or extension leads, Wi-Fi or network connections, and catering. Additionally, you may need a conference bridge number, or an online meeting web link – to connect your attendees. Dependent upon the meeting channel you have chosen (e.g. video conference), a member of your tech support team may be required to assist with the initial set up, and this will require pre-booking, by raising a ticket with IT help desk.

Besides these resources, you should consider any supporting documentation required e.g. an Agenda, PowerPoint presentation, previous Minutes, or any supplementary reports. Your exec can advise you of those specific requirements.

 Consider what resources your meeting requires e.g. a meeting room, Wi-Fi connection, display screen, catering or tech support. Ensure these resources are pre-booked for your meeting.

For the 'Team Project Meeting', the following resources are required:

- A meeting room reservation at the Canary Wharf office between 1400-1500 on 8 April

- Room to be large enough for 6 people with Wi-Fi
- A catering order of tea/coffee/water x 6 for a 1400 arrival
- Flipchart with pad and pens
- A meeting Agenda

The Canary Wharf office is an internal site, and you are already familiar with the meeting rooms, their layout and how to check their availability. Room bookings, catering and meeting support materials (flipchart, pad and pens) are all managed by the Canary Wharf Office Reception Team. You approach the Reception Team with your requirements, and they confirm your booking for the time requested. You have been allocated the 'Pullman Room'. The Reception Team have also confirmed your catering order, the flip chart pad and pens, and that Wi-Fi is operating in the Pullman Room, and have provided you with the Wi-Fi connection code. The Agenda document is something you will need to discuss with your exec, before creating a draft. Ask your exec to approve it, prior to circulation.

 Familiarise yourself with the meeting rooms available at your office location. How many attendees do they accommodate? What AV or presentation tools are available? Which rooms are suitable for a working lunch?

Additional meeting information

In addition to the meeting invitation fields of **To, Subject, Location, Start Time and End Time,** there is a main area, in the invite, where further information can be added. This is referred to as the **body** of the meeting invite. Utilise this space by adding further meeting information, which will assist the attendees. You could include a location map, conference bridge number, agenda (as an embedded file) , minutes, format of meeting, timings per meeting item, video conference code, online connection code or catering arrangements. Of course you don't need to do this for every meeting, but for senior level, more structured meetings, or meetings with larger groups of attendees, you may find this extra space very useful.

For the 'Team Project Meeting' invite, including a location map for the Canary Wharf office will be beneficial. A map of the exact office location, will undoubtedly help visitors who have not visited before, and are not familiar with the location.

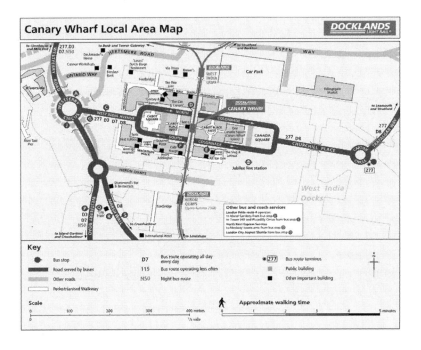

When the Agenda is finalised, I would definitely include it. Adding an Agenda, or previous minutes, to the body of the meeting invite, keeps everything related to that meeting in one place, and shows efficiency and forethought. Sometimes PAs email documents around separately when it isn't required, and best practice would be to embed the Agenda or Minutes within the actual appointment itself. It's easily accessible, aids the attendees to find the relevant data, and saves everyone time by keeping the relevant information together for future reference.

If your executive is not familiar with this practice – suggest it. It's a lot easier for everyone, and you will not be asked for copies of the Agenda, closer to the date, because attendees have forgotten where they filed it. However, if the Agenda is not ready to issue at this stage, it can be added later. You could also add, in the body of the invite, that Wi-Fi will be available and that refreshments are pre-booked.

So to summarise, for the Team Project Meeting we are going to include the following data in the body of the meeting invite:

- Location map of the Canary Wharf Office
- Wi-Fi connection instructions
- Confirmation that tea and coffee will be available
- Confirmation that a flip chart, pad and pens are available
- The meeting Agenda

Remember, that the key meeting information should always be viewable in the meeting fields, and any ancillary or supporting information can be embedded into the meeting invite. Data contained in the fields is viewable at first glance, whereas any information held in the body of the meeting appointment is only viewable when the appointment is opened.

 Obtain information relevant to your office location for future meeting invitations e.g. location map, transport links, nearby parking facilities and rail information.

Issuing the invite

You are now in receipt of all the meeting requirements, you know the attendee availability, the meeting resources have been pre-booked, and you have obtained any additional information for your attendees e.g. the Canary Wharf Office location map and Wi-Fi connection codes. Let's issue the meeting invite.

With Outlook open, select the Calendar link in the bottom left corner of the main window, and open your executive's diary.

Select the meeting date from the calendar top left; the date will become highlighted in light blue. Your main screen view, will now show the date you selected. Ensure you are showing 'work week' view (so you see your exec's working week). The view settings can be amended in the 'view' tab. Double-click in the calendar, at the start time required for the meeting request. An Appointment window will open, type in the subject name and adjust any Start or End times as needed – check the date is accurate.

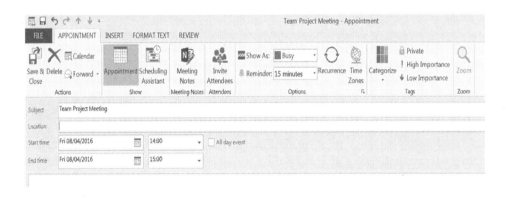

Enter the location of the meeting, type the full address in the body of the invite for those who are not familiar with the Canary Wharf office location. If your meeting location is known to everyone, the full address isn't necessary, and a shortened version is fine. Embed the location map into the main body by clicking in the space, and select insert picture or file. If the majority are driving to the venue, add the postal address for sat nav.

How to schedule a meeting

Continue to add any further information for the attendees - to the main body of the invite e.g. catering arrangements, Wi-Fi connection code, in-room meeting resources, or a contact telephone number. If the meeting you are scheduling is a conference call, you would insert the conference bridge number, together with any additional phone instructions e.g. leader PIN, mute button, toll free or international numbers.

Add to bible...

Obtain your exec's conference bridge number and PIN, plus user instructions, and add to your bible.

If you are scheduling a web based (online) meeting, you should insert the link to the web meeting, together with any additional joining instructions such as audio number and PIN. Finally, insert any accompanying documents such as Agenda, Minutes, or slide deck in PowerPoint format. Use the main body of the invite as the dashboard for the meeting. Everything the attendees need to run that meeting – should be in that space.

131

When your meeting invite is built, it's time to add the attendees. Select the invite attendees button from the top of your screen, and the 'To' field will open

Invite Attendees

up. The window's title will change from Appointment to Meeting once you have added others in the 'To' field. In the 'To' field, begin typing the name of the recipient and Outlook will find the name (if listed in your global address book). By default, Outlook will always look for contacts in the Global Address list. However, if your contact is in **your** address book, select the drop down menu for the Address Book at the top of your screen, and search for your contact. Alternatively, type part of the name in the 'To' field, and select 'check names'.

Add to bible...

Obtain your exec's online meeting login and password, plus user instructions, and add to your bible.

Double-check you have included the correct attendees, and when you are satisfied your meeting invitation is accurate, contains the necessary information, and is without any formatting or spelling errors – hit send.

Scheduling etiquette

As diary management has become more of a skill, a diary **etiquette** has emerged and is commonly observed amongst PAs. This unwritten rule (which I am about to share with you) is a form of politeness, combined with the responsibility of who completes which tasks when scheduling meetings. Using examples, here are some of the rules to observe when scheduling meetings:

✓ Your executive has verbally requested a meeting with the finance director – *it's your responsibility to issue the meeting invite.*
✓ The finance director has requested to meet with your executive – *it's the finance director's responsibility to issue the invite.*

- ✓ A client has requested your exec travels to meet at their offices – *it's the client's responsibility to issue the invite.*
- ✓ A client has requested to meet your exec at your offices – *it's your responsibility to issue the invite, as your office is hosting.*
- ✓ The CEO's office has requested a meeting with your exec – *the CEO's office should issue the meeting invite.*
- ✓ Your exec is interviewing a prospective candidate – *it's the Human Resource department's responsibility to arrange, and issue the meeting invites.*
- ✓ Your exec's first report has requested 1 to 1 time - *it's the first report's responsibility to issue the invite.*
- ✓ A sub-ordinate would like your exec to join their team meeting – *it's the subordinate's responsibility to issue the invite.*
- ✓ Always respond to a meeting invite (accept, decline, tentative) never ignore it.
- ✓ If your exec can no longer attend a meeting – *send their apologies (with the decline option).*
- ✓ If requesting a reschedule – *provide as much notice as possible.*
- ✓ Always issue the invite within 24 hours of agreeing the time/date slot.

Venue finding

Throughout this chapter we've focused on internal meetings – meetings which take place at your company's own location or office. Whilst this is the most cost effective option, on occasion it isn't always possible to host a meeting internally, and you'll need to source an external venue. Situations such as these arise when you are co-ordinating a face to face meeting (perhaps for 16 plus attendees), and you don't have a large enough meeting room at your disposal. There will also be larger company events (with their own event budget) which dictate that you should take the meeting offsite, such as your annual kick off meeting, leadership group strategy day, business development away day, or the annual company conference. These 'large scale' events are great for PAs to really showcase their event management skills. A lot of planning and co-ordination goes into a successful event, and your hard work will be noticed, deservedly so, when you've met your brief, come in under budget, and everything has run smoothly on the day.

Once you've obtained your brief from your executive, regarding your offsite event, the first thing to consider is the venue. How many attendees (or delegates), are being invited? Does it require an overnight stay? What budget do you have for conference space and hotel accommodation? Will the meeting take place close to your office location? Or midpoint between 2 of your office locations? Or in another part of the country which is situated near to your operational or development teams? Consider where your delegates are based - prior to choosing the location for the meeting. Where do the majority of delegates live? If necessary, map out the names of your delegates, and next to their names write the city in which they live (or are closest to). You will soon see a pattern emerging, and will be able to pin point the city which is the most convenient to host your event. By identifying a location which is easily accessible to most, you will reduce travel costs (from your overall budget) and travel time (for your delegates).

With your event location identified, the next step is finding your event venue. Venues are not just restricted to hotels, there are a variety of distinctive venues out there to choose from, and ones that will match the brief and style of your event. Consider academic venues, such as universities and colleges, or sporting venues for large scale conferences and meetings. Unique venues such as an historic castle, old manor house or country estate. And contemporary venues in city centre locations e.g. the Gherkin, the Shard, Tower 42 or City Hall. Of course you may prefer the traditional hotel option, and this may be the best solution if you are hosting your delegates overnight. Venue finding can be a time consuming task, and venue finding agencies exist which can support you with your quest, purportedly for free. But be careful they are not receiving a commission from chosen venues, and are therefore not providing independent or unbiased advice. There are also various venue finding websites providing online search facilities, but again, these will not necessarily provide you with a comprehensive selection of venues, only the venues who have signed up to that particular website.

Many major cities in the UK and around the world will have a **convention bureau**. Sometimes they have a different name and may be known as a conference office, destination management organisation or convention and visitor bureau. Whatever they're called, they exist to promote their city as a place to hold meetings, conferences and business events, and to support meeting planners throughout the organising process. Such organisations offer FREE and impartial advice, often providing a full venue finding service, bid assistance, planning toolkits and promotional materials. In the UK, Visit Bristol is a good example of such a service, and has a dedicated conference team, to support meetings and events organisers.

LET US FIND YOUR IDEAL VENUE

BRISTOL

Why Bristol?

- International airport with over 110 connections
- Two mainline railway stations
- Easy access from M4 & M5 motorways
- Walkable range of venues within compact city centre
- Amazing and unique venues
- Conference capacity in excess of 1,000
- More than 2,000 four-star bedrooms

Why Us?

- **FREE** venue finding service
- Organisation of delegate accommodation
- Special rates for train travel
- Impartial and expert knowledge

Email: conference@destinationbristol.co.uk   **Tel:** +44 (0)117 946 2200   **Destination**Bristol
www.visitbristol.co.uk/conference

Some conference bureaus have great deals and offers available, for meeting co-ordinators to take advantage of, e.g. reduced rail fares, discounted day delegate rates and seasonal packages.

Next time you are sourcing an external venue, contact your relevant conference bureau, and share your event brief with them. They will respond with a completely independent and comprehensive selection of venues, and can often support with rate negotiation and online accommodation bookings.

Visit Bristol's conference team publish an annual venue directory, featuring all of the key venues and their capacity. Approach your local conference bureau and ask what publications are available. Familiarise yourself with what's available in your immediate vicinity.

Meeting terminology

Do you know your 1 to 1 from your Kick Off? Your briefing from your mop up? Or are you feeling Confused.com? Meeting invites can often contain meeting terminology which sound like it could be a military code. But fear not – refer to the definitions in the table, and you too can talk the talk of your business associates.

Meeting terminology explained

Term	Definition
1 to 1	1 to 1s also known as One to Ones, 121s, One on Ones, are individual meetings between 2 people. Often between a manager and their direct report. Content will include general updates, review and prioritisation of tasks. 1 to 1s provide an opportunity to talk through key issues and agree strategy.
Advisory Group	An informal group with an advisory role. It may look and act like a committee but is unlikely to be constituted or accountable.
AGM	Annual General Meeting - the governing document of an organisation will say whether or not an AGM has to be held, and should set out the rules the organisation has to follow for its AGM. All members are usually eligible to attend. An AGM is a meeting that a business or organization has every year, to discuss issues and elect new officials.
Assembly	A meeting of people who represent different parts of a large organization.
Audio Conference	A way of holding a meeting or discussion in which people are connected by telephone.
Board Meeting	A meeting of the board of directors.
Briefing	A meeting or document in which people receive information or instructions.
Catch Up	Similar to a 1 to 1 but with someone other than a direct report.

Committee	A person or group of people elected or appointed to perform some service or function, as to investigate, report on, or act upon a particular matter.
Conference	A large meeting, often lasting a few days, where individuals meet to discuss a specific topic or theme.
Conference Call	A telephone call which allows three or more people to take part at the same time.
De-briefing	A meeting where someone gives a report about an important job or project that they have just finished. Or a meeting to discuss a client meeting, after the client has departed, with internal colleagues.
EGM	Extraordinary General Meeting. EGMs might be called for special business that arises in between AGMs - e.g. amending the governing document/ closing the organisation/making a decision on something outside the existing powers of the committee etc.
Executive Team	The senior management, executive management, or management team of the company. Generally a team of individuals at the highest level of organizational management who have the day-to-day responsibilities of managing a company or corporation (also known as leadership group).
Focus Group	When problem-solving, focus groups are where several experts or informed individuals share their point of view on a specific topic or problem.
Forum	An organized event or meeting at which people discuss a specific topic.
General Meeting	A meeting of members of the organisation. An organisation with members will probably have to hold a general meeting at least once a year (Annual General Meeting). General meetings involve all the members, not just the committee. If other General Meetings are held in between, they may be called Extraordinary or Special General Meetings. Rules for calling and holding General Meetings should be set out in the Governing Document.

Kick-Off	**The first meeting with the project team and the client of the project. This meeting would follow definition of the base elements for the project and other project planning activities. A gathering of interested parties to discuss a plan or strategy before launching a program or project.**
Management Meeting	A meeting involving the senior management team.
Mop up	Similar to a debrief but focusing on the actions which are still outstanding.
Off-site	An external meeting, away from company premises. Also called an 'offsite retreat' if involving overnight accommodation, and known as an 'Away day' meeting in the UK.
Seminar	A conference or other meeting for discussion or training.
SGM	Special General Meeting - see General Meeting.
Steering Group	A group of people who are responsible for monitoring a company's operations or project progress, by ensuring it complies with company policies, including resources and costs. Often focusing on corporate governance.
Sub Committee	Governing Documents will set out whether or not a committee may delegate powers and decision making to sub groups, and what rules apply. If the Governing Document does not give this power, then committees cannot delegate. Companies have to follow Company Law in setting up and running sub groups. See also Working Group.
Team Meeting	A meeting between a manager and their team.
Town Hall	Meetings which involve all employees, often used as a communication briefing. Town halls encourage questions and input from attendees. Usually held at each office location. They are informal, corporate gatherings used to share information such as business results or personnel changes.
Video-conference	Technology that allows users in different locations to hold face-to-face meetings, without having to move to a single location. This technology is particularly

	convenient for business users in different cities, or even different countries because it saves the time, expense and hassle associated with business travel. Uses for video conferencing include holding routine meetings, negotiating business deals, interviewing job candidates and connecting multiple sites for regional meetings.
Water Cooler	An Americanism referring to time spent chatting at the water cooler in an office. Studies have proved how productive that is amongst colleagues. Now used to name virtual, regular, team catch up meetings. The meeting is unstructured and informal, and aims to replicate the water cooler conversation, but for colleagues who are remote.
Webinar	A seminar or other presentation that takes place online, allowing participants in different locations to see and hear the presenter, ask questions, and sometimes answer polls. Each participant uses their own computer to connect to the presenter.
Working Group	A committee may appoint a working group to go away and do tasks e.g. planning an event, writing a policy or funding application, which would take up too much time in the main committee. Working groups are not formal groups, and should not be given any decision making powers but should bring everything back to the committee for decisions.

6

Professional Associations

What's in this chapter?

The majority of industries have a professional body (or association), to represent the profession, maintain standards, and address key issues in that particular sector. There are numerous associations in existence, for example, the Chartered Institute of Marketing is the body for marketing and business development professionals in the UK, and the Institute of Directors is a UK association for company directors, senior business leaders and entrepreneurs. Each professional association, binds professionals working in that particular specialism, and offers support to its members.

An association is usually a **not for profit** organisation, and most often run by members for its members, offering training and development, and levels of certification, for professional skills and achievements. Members are charged an annual membership fee, with different fee structures, depending on the level of membership required. Membership is only granted, by the association, if the applicant has been successful in their application.

You may wish to consider joining a professional association for PAs, in addition to doing your own business networking, or joining a local PA networking group (which is covered in Chapter 7). In this chapter, we will review professional associations for PAs, the benefits of joining, and which associations are available globally.

- Professional associations – an introduction
- Benefits of joining a professional association
- Choosing your professional association
- Levels of membership
- Membership application
- Professional associations across the globe

Professional associations – an introduction

Professional associations have evolved considerably over the last couple of decades, and are more user friendly and accessible than ever before, thanks to the internet. Training resources can be sourced online, networking opportunities are available at the touch of a keystroke, and past publications and newsletters can be downloaded within seconds. The internet revolution has transformed professional associations into a valuable online resource. Associations often communicate industry developments as they happen, and also provide members with the opportunity to network with their peers online. As a general rule, associations publish monthly or fortnightly newsletters via email, offer industry related discounts to members, promote and provide training solutions, and share best practices.

A common misconception is that you **do not** have to be an experienced PA to join a professional association. Associations exist to support PA students, as equally as they support experienced PAs furthering their careers. The majority of associations provide a multitude of training courses, either facilitated internally or in partnership with an external training provider. Choose from online, self-study or class led courses. Courses are often discounted for members, as opposed to purchasing direct with a training provider. Courses are specifically chosen to aid your career development as a PA, so review the training options available with your professional association, and understand which courses are on trend within your sector.

Professional associations can be a fantastic resource for everything related to your career, and I recommend joining an association to aid you on your journey as a PA. If you are dedicated to progressing your career, want to keep abreast of industry changes, and are keen to network with fellow PAs, then membership will provide you with the appropriate platform. These are **not for profit** organisations, so membership shouldn't break the bank, and listing membership on your CV and LinkedIn page will boost your credentials.

Benefits of joining a professional association

Perhaps you are already a member of a professional association, and are benefiting from the opportunities and resources it provides. Fantastic! If not, maybe you are considering joining an association but are uncertain what membership will provide. What are the particular benefits of joining an association? Is it worth the annual membership fee? Are there member events in your immediate vicinity? Will membership aid you on your career journey, and increase your employment or promotion opportunities? Industry associations have a core theme of benefits available to members. Benefits can vary, depending upon the association, but generally include:

- Networking opportunities
- Leaning and development
- Recruitment
- Recognition
- Access to supplier discounts
- Industry news and resources

Benefits explained

Networking opportunities	These may include online networking with PA members, access to a member's network directory or a forum for members (where members can post a question on the association's website and respond with advice to a previously posted question). In addition to online networking opportunities, associations' co-ordinate face to face events, including annual conferences, summits, seminars, guest speaker events, lunches, evening drinks and additional social gatherings. In conjunction with preferred partners, associations may invite members to supplier events and product launches e.g. hotel launches, conference centre showarounds, airport tours, team event awareness days, car rental fleet promos, corporate gift company promotions, and venue viewings etc.
Learning and development	Associations pride themselves in offering tailored, relevant, and accessible training courses to their members. Courses are offered across different channels including live webinars, on demand webinars, downloadable courses for self-study, and class based trainer courses. Subjects may include career development, improving communications, meeting and event management, project and administration management, MS Office skills, business writing and document layout. Further courses include: improving your grammar, essential PA skills, producing presentations and running effective meetings etc. The range of courses and learning channels available are vast! You will find something to suit your own style of learning. If you cannot travel into a city hub for class based courses, having access to an online learning resource is invaluable. Courses are available via various online channels including webcast, webinar and downloadable format. However, courses are often chargeable, so consider the costs and value before selection.

	The annual conference and periodic seminars hosted by your chosen association will, almost certainly, contain an element of learning and development opportunities in the event programme. Annual conferences, for example, carry a heavy educational programme with access to workshops, and key note speakers. Attending an annual conference will also bring you up to date with key industry developments, and create awareness of new products and services. Meet your peers, make new contacts and learn from leading industry professionals.
Recruitment	Are you looking for a new PA position? Are you aware that recruiters place vacancy ads directly with professional associations? Well, they do! It's another avenue to explore when considering your next career move. Professional associations encourage employers to advertise job vacancies exclusively on their websites, therefore inviting suitable employers to connect with the target market of professional, intelligent and career focused PAs. These vacancies are viewable by members only, so you may hear about a fantastic new position before it's even been uploaded onto a general recruitment website. Find your perfect job by browsing the jobs listed on your association's website. Remember to check the job boards of your professional association first. You will be pleasantly surprised by the volume and quality of vacancies listed. Associations also publish online salary surveys, provide further career guidance (via featured articles and searchable content) and provide tips on refreshing your CV.

Recognition	Membership of a professional association confirms your commitment, and dedicated professionalism, as a PA. It is confirmation of your status and industry experience. Upon successful completion and acceptance of your membership application, a membership certificate will be posted to you, which you can proudly display at home or in your office. Announce your professional membership on your LinkedIn page, include it on your CV, and mention it in face to face interviews. Be proud that you have achieved recognition for the work you do, and the professional career which you have chosen as a PA.
Access to supplier discounts	Associations commonly partner a number of suppliers in order to promote their goods and services to members, whilst offering specially negotiated discounts. The partnership is mutually beneficial, in that suppliers can reach out to the professional PA environment, and the PA enjoys the reduced fees and introductory rates. Suppliers will vary from large international companies, to small local independents, but all will be approved by the association for providing a relevant PA product or service. As an example of discounts available, professional PA associations around the globe, are currently offering members discounted services for: private driver hire, health insurance, gourmet gifts and florist services. Travel insurance, hotel room rates, wine merchants goods, entertainment and legal assistance. Further discounts on offer include fashion items, restaurant vouchers, and health and beauty products. Discounts are also available for training courses and training materials, including self-study and reference books, and discounted PA magazine subscriptions.
Industry news and resources	Member's online areas are a wealth of information, resources and tips. You will find a library of previously published association newsletters, features and articles. Search for specific online task tips including: meeting and event planning checklists, document templates, MS

Office tips, business writings skills guides, keyboard shortcuts, and time management solutions. Download journals, review career advice, read articles on new products, industry changes and trends. Review featured articles from industry professionals, and external contributors.

Find inspiration for your career development, research learning and development opportunities, and update your knowledge with the very latest news and developments in your sector.

Choosing your professional association

There are numerous professional associations across the globe, and certainly too many to list in this chapter. However, a comprehensive list of professional associations can be found at: **www.executivesecretary.com/associations.** The majority of organisations communicate online, or through a restricted web portal, so you could effectively join the Institute of UK Legal Secretaries and PAs, if you are based overseas (should you choose to). So, you are not limited to joining an association which is local to you geographically, the focus is upon joining the relevant professional association for your career and sector. Remember that inspiration and education can be gleaned from an association overseas - if there isn't a suitable association local to you. International associations exist which have thousands of members, and this can mean better resources, and training opportunities for members, due to bigger budgets. On the flipside, smaller associations may offer a more personal touch, co-ordinate events in your region, and facilitate training courses in your area. Weigh up the benefits of joining a large international association, versus a group which is closer to you.

Before committing to membership, review and compare several organisations in your particular employment sector. Is your chosen PA sector legal, medical, financial or educational? Private or public sector? Which association is of the most interest to you, offers increased benefits to members, updates its website frequently with new material, and is interesting and informative?

Use the checklist on the next page to complete your research, and determine which association is the right fit for you. When you have found a membership body which suits all your requirements, and fits your budget, sign up and await your welcome pack, and member's certificate. Oh – and don't forget to frame it and hang it somewhere prominent!

If financial constraints prevent you from joining a professional association, then focus your attention on various networking groups instead. Membership is free, there are a multitude of groups in existence, and you can join as many as is necessary to suit your requirements.

The UK in particular, has a wealth of fantastic networking groups in London, and nationwide. The benefits of joining a PA networking group, can be just as beneficial as joining a professional association, and is often fee free. See Chapter 7 for further networking ideas.

Levels of membership

Memberships of professional associations are offered at different levels, so find your level of entry before applying. As a general rule the membership levels are:

Level	Description
Student	Entry level e.g. for anyone who is training to be or wants to be a personal assistant.
Affiliate	Second level of membership, for newly qualified and junior level PAs e.g. minimum number of 2 years in the role with foundation level qualifications.
Associate/ Member	Third tier of membership available to those with considerably more experience in the role. PAs who have obtained an increased number of years of service, with an intermediate level qualification.
Fellow	Fellowship is reserved for those who are experts in their field. Fellowship is the ultimate membership level obtainable. You will have met the criteria for a total number of years in the business, attained seniority in your profession with an impressive career history, and have an advanced level qualification. Fellowship demonstrates the highest level of recognition, achievement and contribution to the PA profession.
Corporate	Corporate membership is purchased by the employer, for its employees. For example, if a large company with 20 PAs wants its PAs to benefit from a professional association membership, it is cost effective to purchase a group membership, instead of purchasing 20 individual memberships.

Membership application

Your chosen professional association will stipulate which supporting documents they require, in order to process your application. Usually this consists of completing an application form, together with evidence of your qualifications, your CV, plus the fee. This is so that the association can vet your qualifications, career history, and compatibility with the association's objectives, and membership requirements.

Professional associations often offer corporate memberships in addition to individual memberships. Joining as a collective group, within a company, can be more cost effective. The benefits of joining will be greater, as you can share experiences with your peers, and attend networking and conference events together.

If you are employed by a large company which employs several administrative professionals, ask your employer if they are a corporate member of a professional administration association. If not, ask your employer to consider corporate membership, and explain the employee benefits. Champion the requirement for your employer to join an association, and raise awareness with your peers.

Add to bible...

Add details of your professional association to your bible. List the annual conference date, and any courses which interest you. Note any regional events or social evenings which you'd like to attend.

Professional associations across the globe

Let's view a snapshot of professional PA associations across the globe, to see what's available.

Association of Medical Secretaries, Practice Managers, Administrators and Receptionists (AMSPAR)

Sector: Medical

HQ: UK

Contact: info@amspar.com   www.amspar.co.uk

Training courses available in partnership with City & Guilds.

The Association of Medical Secretaries, Practice Managers, Administrators and Receptionists (AMSPAR) was established in 1964, with the aim of creating and promoting appropriate qualifications, initially for those working as medical secretaries, and subsequently for medical receptionists, administrators and practice managers. AMSPAR is a professional association which recognises both formal qualifications, and length of service in a healthcare environment. AMSPAR members currently receive special privileges and services, including access to a free legal helpline, a range of professional guidelines on a wide number of healthcare and employment topics, in addition to work and non-work related discounts. AMSPAR works with City & Guilds to provide a range of nationally recognised qualifications, suitable for delivery as either full or part time study programmes.

Ask your peers and PA contacts if they are a member of a professional association. What variety of benefits have they experienced, and would they recommend joining? Do they consider it value for money?

British Society of Medical Secretaries and Administrators (BSMSA)

Sector: Medical

HQ: UK

Contact: liz.wilson@bsmsa.org.uk   www.bsmsa.org.uk

Training courses available in partnership with City & Guilds.

The BSMSA was founded in 1983 by two working medical secretaries. Since then it has grown into an organisation representing medical secretaries, PAs, clinical team secretaries, administrators and clerical staff working in the NHS,

General, Academic, Private Practice and Primary Care. BSMSA membership is open to all medical secretaries, PAs and administrative staff, as well as those with a general interest in the society, across the NHS and Private Practice. The BSMSA provides introductory and continuous training courses, professional support and a chance to meet and exchange views at local and national meetings, and through the BSMSA's newsletter and Facebook page.

Check your employee handbook for a policy covering professional subscriptions. You may be entitled to join a professional association, and expense back the annual membership fee. If this isn't evident in your employee handbook, ask your local HR representative for guidance.

American Society of Administrative Professionals (ASAP)

Sector: General
HQ: US
Contact: info@asaporg.com
Training courses available.

www.asaporg.com

The American Society of Administrative Professionals was established in 2005, to provide year-round online professional development, training, and resources - to address the changing roles and demanding responsibilities of Administrative Professionals and Executive Assistants. There are more than 60,000 ASAP members in North America and around the world. Membership to ASAP is FREE, and includes access to articles and columns focusing on business skills and career development, the popular monthly FastTrack newsletter, and "Learn It in a Minute" videos. Members also have access to hundreds of online training courses, live and on-demand webinars. Additionally, ASAP members have the opportunity to participate in a prestigious certification program, PACE, the Professional Administrative Certificate of Excellence.

The International Association of Administrative Professionals (IAAP)

Sector: General
HQ: US
Contact: amy.randolph@iaap-hq.org
Training courses available.

www.iaap-hq.org

IAAP (International Association of Administrative Professionals) is a not-for-profit professional association for administrative professionals. IAAP strives to ensure individuals working in office and administrative professions have the opportunity to connect, learn, lead, and excel. The association founded in 1942 as the National Secretaries Association, to provide a professional network and educational resource for secretarial staff. The association's name was changed in 1998 to the International Association of Administrative Professionals to encompass the large number of varied administrative job titles, and recognize the advancing role of administrative support staff.

Association of Secretaries and Administrative Professionals in Asia Pacific (ASA)

Sector: All Administration
HQ: Philippines

ASIA PACIFIC

www.asapap.org

The Association of Secretaries and Administrative Professionals in Asia Pacific (ASA) was founded in 1974 by the Philippine Association of Secretaries, to provide an opportunity for secretaries in and around Asia to meet and share their knowledge and experience. Today ASA is the regional platform for Asia Pacific professional associations. Its members include associations representing Indonesia, Singapore, India, Malaysia, China, Pakistan, Japan, Sri-Lanka, Brunei, and Korea.

The Australian Institute of Office Professionals (AIOP)

Sector: General
HQ: Australia
Contact: membership@aiop.com.au
Training courses available.

www.aiop.com.au

The Australian Institute of Office Professionals represents office professionals in Australia. Office Professionals are people employed to carry out an administrative role in a professional capacity, and can include a broad range of roles in all aspects of a business such as managers, team leaders, project officers, executive/personal assistants, and administrative support officers etc. Professional and personal development meetings are held regularly in Chapters around Australia. Anyone involved with the office/administrative profession is encouraged to become a member and attend a local meeting.

The Association of Administrative Professionals New Zealand (AAPNZ)

Sector: General
HQ: New Zealand
Contact: membership@aapnz.org.nz
Training courses available.

www.aapnz.org.nz

The Association of Administrative Professionals New Zealand Incorporated (AAPNZ Inc) is a voluntary national association administered by its members, for its members. Our membership includes executive assistants, personal assistants, administration managers, receptionists, call centre operators, accounts staff, school secretaries, industry trainers, etc - anyone involved either full or part time in administrative professional roles, in any industry. This is a supportive local and national network which will give administrative professionals opportunities for personal growth, and career development. Members are based throughout New Zealand as well as overseas.

Executive Assistant Network (EAN)

Sector: All Administration
HQ: Australia
Contact: admin@executiveassistant.com
Training courses available.

www.executiveassistant.com

The Network is designed for leading executive and personal assistants, working for board level executives or general management level executives, in the top corporations in Australia, and now also around the world. EAN is a fun, interactive and social business membership organisation, designed to ensure members are better equipped to provide the levels of support needed. The objectives of EAN's member's network, website, education and training initiatives, are to help EAs and PAs to become more efficient and proficient in their roles. These objectives are met through a combination of web based tools, guides, directories, chat rooms, member to member communication tools, networking functions and literally hundreds of education initiatives including courses, retreats, mentor programs, discussion groups and conferences.

Caribbean Association of Administrative Professionals (CAAP)

Sector: All Administration
HQ: Rotates across the Caribbean Communities

Contact: membership@aaa.ca

www.aaa.ca

The Caribbean Association of Administrative Professionals (CAAP) is the umbrella body for member Associations in the various CARICOM countries, as well as the wider Caribbean area. Current member countries of CAAP are: Aruba, Barbados, Dominica, Guyana, Jamaica, St. Kitts and Nevis, Trinidad and Tobago, Turks and Caicos. CAAP is committed to the objective of its motto "united towards a better world", and envisages a vibrant organization embracing all secretaries and administrative professionals, forging links which surmount political considerations and jealousies; and raising to new heights the standard of the profession in the region.

Association of Administrative Assistants (AAA)

Sector: All Administration
HQ: Canada
Contact: contact@aaa.ca
Training courses available.

www.aaa.ca

The Association of Administrative Assistants is a voluntary Canadian chartered, non-profit organization, administered by its members for its members. Consisting of office assistants and professionals from a wide variety of roles and titles, the Association assists members in the continuing development of administrative skills and professional growth, resulting in increased employment opportunities and advancement in the workplace. Membership in an association such as ours, provides access to professional development opportunities, knowledge and information specific to your role, and networking opportunities with colleagues from across Canada. This gives you a sense of connection whether you work in a small, medium, large or home-based office.

Ask your chosen professional association how many training courses are inclusive (if any) in the annual membership fee. Courses can be expensive so consider what your association provides, inclusive of the membership fee.

NB At the time of writing, the UK has a newly launched association: EPAA, which is the new national body for Executive and Personal Assistants.

7

Business Networking

What's in this Chapter?

We'll be focusing on business networking and looking at the various channels of networking available e.g. online, internal (within your corporation) and external (outside of your corporation). We'll explore the specific benefits of business networking as a personal assistant, and how to build contacts and peer to peer relationships. Learn how to join a regional networking group, and discover hints and tips for attending your first networking group event. Furthermore, we'll be looking at extending your network reach by considering global networking groups, reviewing the groups in existence, and paving the way to making PA contacts in New York, Brisbane, Paris and the world!

Networking is vital for today's business savvy PA, work your way through the components in this chapter, and you will soon be networking with ease and reaping the rewards.

- Business networking – an introduction
- Benefits of networking
- Building relationships
- Information exchange
- Internal business networking
- The personal assistant directory
- External business networking
- Meeting suppliers
- Career opportunities
- UK PA networking groups
- Global PA networking groups
- Attending your first networking event

Business networking – an introduction

"Networking is defined as the act of making contact and exchanging information with other people, groups and institutions, to develop mutually beneficial relationships". *Yourdictionary.com*

"A supportive system of sharing information and services among individuals, and groups having a common interest." *Dictionary.com*.

"Creating a group of acquaintances and associates and keeping it active, through regular communication for mutual benefit. Networking is based on the question 'How can I help?' and not 'What can I get?'" *BusinessDictionary.com*

You will observe that the common theme in the definitions above, is the **connection** of a group of likeminded people, to **share knowledge** and **exchange information** for mutual benefit.

As we discussed in Chapter 6, professional PA associations exist which will offer business networking opportunities to members. However, there are specialist 'networking groups' which co-exist (independently of professional associations), which support and connect PAs on their career journeys. The fundamental difference between the two, is that professional associations are a structured and governed body, providing annual membership for an annual fee, operated by a dedicated board of directors, with a formal calendar of events and various training solutions. A business networking group, whilst also focusing on a specialist career sector, is less formal. There will be no annual joining fee, perhaps a fee to attend individual events only. The group encourages a social element for members to meet face to face, and may arrange talks and presentations from leading industry contributors. The emphasis is on communicating with likeminded professional individuals in your sector, and more often than not, making new contacts and friends in your immediate location. Business networking is also a gateway, allowing you to give something back to your sector, share knowledge and ideas with your peers, ask for advice, and discuss experiences.

Networking opportunities are also present in our day to day lives. Consider the relationships you have with friends and family. Have you recently received an invitation to a family lunch, a friend's party or a social club event? Attending such events places you into direct, face to face, contact with your family and friends. This is an established network and provides you with the perfect opportunity to ask questions, and bounce ideas off your personal contacts. People who know you well, will do their utmost to share their personal advice, knowledge and guidance. Whilst this particular type of networking is not often associated with business networking it's still extremely important, and you can practise your networking skills in a safe environment, whilst boosting your confidence and gathering information. Let's look at the benefits of business networking in further detail.

Benefits of networking

Do you work for a large or small organisation? How many colleagues do you connect with on a day to day basis? Do you often chat to colleagues at the water cooler, in the café, or at the vending machine? Then you are already networking within your organisation. Impromptu conversations with colleagues who you do not work closely with can, and often does, reveal news and information which is extremely insightful and useful.

Active networking is important to career development. Often confused with selling, networking is actually about building long-term relationships and expanding your existing contacts. It involves meeting and getting to know people who you can assist, and who can potentially help you in return. Business networking is a really valuable way to expand your knowledge, learn from the success of others, meet other PAs in the business and improve upon your social skills as an individual.

As a PA, business networking is not about selling a product or service, it's about communicating with other PAs and connecting with a network of advisors, colleagues, friends and joining a community. Regular networking will improve your confidence, boost your self-esteem, push your own personal boundaries, and give you satisfaction for helping others. PA networks provide a gateway for sharing best practice information and discovering business techniques, used in organisations external to your own.

Building relationships

Attending a networking event can provide you with a great source of connections, and opens the door to talk to highly influential people that you wouldn't otherwise be able to talk to, or meet, in your day to day activities. For example, you could come into contact with prominent business leaders, company CEOs, executive level PAs, award winning PAs, motivational speakers and industry experts. It's a forum for connecting people that would not usually come together, but could be great connections for you throughout your career. Attending a face to face networking event will also introduce you to PAs in different sectors, all under one roof e.g. PAs working in financial services, medicine, gas or oil, virtual assistants and education. Legal PAs, government assistants, administrators, PAs in entertainment, travel and media, public and commercial sectors. Head teacher's assistants, Board level executive assistants, trainee legal assistants and celebrity assistants! The scope of meeting interesting people, working in different environments to your own, is huge.

Networking groups often invite representatives from local recruitment agencies, training providers and hotel managers to talk at PA events, give presentations and be on hand for general industry tips and advice. So, it's a gentle introduction to enable you to build your relationships with new suppliers and business professionals, without any of the 'hard sell'.

When you get to the end of the day or, week, review emails in your Outlook sent folder. Who was a new connection this week? Recognise the individuals who are new worthwhile contacts, and send them a request to connect via LinkedIn. Connecting via LinkedIn establishes and reaffirms your business connection. Furthermore, whenever a personal connection on LinkedIn changes employment, you will still hold the most up to date contact details and will be able to connect with that person. Contact details on LinkedIn can sometimes be more reliable than the details in your Outlook folder.

Information exchange

A PA network can be an excellent source of new perspectives and ideas to help you in your role. Exchanging information on common challenges, experiences and goals, is a key benefit of networking because it allows you to gain new insights that you may not have otherwise considered. For instance, discover which expense management systems are used by your peers and why. Which travel management company is favoured by the large corporates, and what is the common opinion on the latest smartphone or tablet device in relation to diary management.

The answers to such questions, although not commercially sensitive, are unlikely to be published or available online. However, by asking your PA contacts in your networking group, whether face to face or online, you will be able to find the answers. Obtaining feedback on back office systems and software from experienced PAs in other companies, is an invaluable insight. Particularly, if your organisation is experiencing issues in that specific area. If appropriate, forward any useful information and industry developments to the relevant department at your organisation, who will appreciate your input.

Having like-minded PAs to talk to, across different sectors, also gives you the opportunity to gain advice from them on all sorts of things, related to your own career or even your personal life. It doesn't have to focus on business! You could ask for local information or advice, during a face to face networking event. For example, you are new to the area, still settling in and want to improve your knowledge of your new surroundings. There is a drinks event for PAs after work, at a nearby 5* hotel next week, and you've decided to attend. Use your recent move as the starting point for conversation e.g. ask attendees at the event where the best restaurant in town is, which is the most reliable cab company, and which sports or leisure facility would they recommend.

Alternatively, you are new to your sector and are struggling with specialist terminology and acronyms in law, finance or medicine. Identify an experienced PA in law, finance or medicine, within your networking group. Approach them and ask for their advice on getting to grips with the unfamiliar business language, and acronyms. Similarly, offering helpful ideas and advice to less experienced PAs, is an excellent way to build your reputation and boost your profile and self-esteem.

As well as approaching PAs in your local business network, perhaps you want to tap into knowledge from a PA in another country. For example, you are based in London, and your business executive is travelling to a conference in Miami Beach, Florida, to deliver a key note speech. You have sourced the flights and hotel online, but don't know which limo company to use for the airport transfers. There are too many to choose from online, and you really want a reputable company for a late night transfer. So ask a PA in Miami – seriously! Join one of the global PA online network groups on LinkedIn, and post the question online. Someone in that network will answer. Remember, that local knowledge is always superior to remote online research, so if you can tap into local knowledge – do.

Global networking groups exist to connect individuals for this purpose, and the benefits of global networking and exchanging information can be mutual. For example, the Miami PA is pleased to have had the opportunity to help someone thousands of miles away, you've tapped into local knowledge through your networking skills and increased your global suppliers list. Furthermore, your business executive receives a seamless transfer from Miami Airport to the hotel, and is grateful to you for your meticulous attention to detail and ingenuity. The Miami PA now has you saved as a contact and will contact you direct for UK tips, when her boss is travelling to London in 6 weeks' time. (Find more information on global networking groups later in this chapter).

Internal business networking

A key element of a PAs success, is having the right contacts and suppliers. Contacts will include key people within your organisation, such as IT specialists, HR administrators, Payroll, Facilities, in house Caterers and Receptionists. Department heads, the Office Manager, peer PAs and members of the Marketing team. These are your key **internal contacts** and building relationships with colleagues in these departments - is another example of networking. To maximise your efficiency, it's essential to have good contacts across most departments. Particularly, in support departments such as IT,

Finance and Facilities. Having a 'go to person' will aid you when your executive's laptop requires a rebuild, a smartphone needs upgrading or an expense claim is late for payment.

 If you are new to your organisation you must identify your key contacts quickly, to establish your network. Locate your internal employee directory and organisation charts, and highlight who you need to reach out to.

Work through the highlighted names, and contact each individual with an introductory email. Ensure your email signature is populated with your full contact details first. When a reply is received, save the sender's details to your Outlook contacts folder for future reference. The reason for connecting via email is twofold. It's unobtrusive as an introduction, and as such, will more than likely generate a positive and welcome response. Secondly, receiving the response via email is a great way of getting that person's contact details directly into your inbox, for saving into your contacts folder.

If you work for a large global organisation, where your colleagues are based all around the world, extending your internal network is equally as important. For instance, you are based in the London office, and your company has offices in New York and Boston. Are you aware of who your peers are in those offices? Do you have a company intranet site (see example over) where you can complete such research? If not, is there an HR Administrator in the US who could steer you in the right direction? Connecting with PAs across the business, is vital for many points of contact. It aids with appointment scheduling, sourcing information quickly, obtaining approvals, submitting reports, and prompting for deadlines. Also, sharing best practice, understanding key company developments, and raises awareness of office moves and internal restructures.

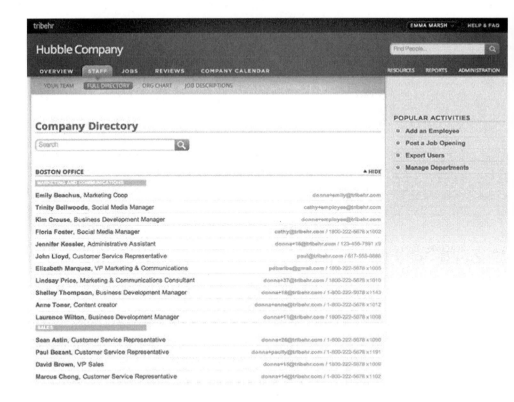

The requirement to approach your internal network can sometimes occur unexpectedly. Here follows a personal account of such a situation. I co-ordinated a business trip, for a previous employer, where 2 group board level executives (VIPs) were visiting from Boston and attending our operational site in Scotland. The CEO UK (my manager) had travelled to Glasgow to host them. I had arranged for a private driver to transfer them from the Blythswood Hotel at 0900 to our site in central Glasgow, then onwards to an offsite meeting commencing at 1100. I received a text message at 1000 that morning, advising that the 2 VIPs would like to buy cashmere, and could I fit that into the Itinerary? I reviewed the itinerary which I had built, identified a 15 minute window between departing the central Glasgow site at 1030, and arriving at the next Glasgow location at 1100. Thankfully, I had factored in 15 minutes contingency time, thinking that the internal site visit would overrun. I texted my boss back confirming "yes it's possible, details to follow".

168

Having no personal knowledge of where to purchase cashmere from in Glasgow (I was based in the South West of England), the first thing I did was to consult the internet. Many Glasgow cashmere shops returned in my search, but which was the best? A window of 15 minutes would not allow for error. I had to locate the best stocked, best located and most suitable Cashmere outlet in Glasgow and I had to find it fast!

As an obvious choice, I called the Tourist Information Office in Glasgow and asked for their advice. After considering my request, the customer service advisor gave me the name of a Cashmere outlet close to Glasgow central station. Reviewing the location of this outlet on Google maps, meant that the driver would have to take a detour from the pre-arranged route. I was also concerned that there would be increased levels of traffic around the station which could cause further delay, not to mention the one way traffic system. I decided this wasn't the most appropriate store to choose logistically. Time was ticking away and this research had eaten up 15 minutes already.

I needed to find a store enroute, or as close as, within the next couple of minutes as the party were due to leave the first Glasgow meeting in 15 minutes time. I needed superior local knowledge, and the only way this could be achieved was by connecting with my internal network.

I contacted my colleague Stacey, on Glasgow Reception, who is very efficient and approachable. I asked the question of Stacey, explained the urgency and much to my relief, Stacey advised that there were 2 Cashmere outlets on the same street in Glasgow with excellent reputations. The street location was also enroute to the next meeting. I figured if one store didn't stock the cashmere goods the VIPs wished to procure, the other outlet would. I thanked Stacey for her invaluable information and local knowledge, and telephoned the information to the executive car. I found myself on speakerphone, providing the store locations to the driver as the car was now in motion with all executives on board. Twenty minutes later, I received a text message from my boss "Cashmere mission successful, 2 items purchased apiece! On time and on way to next meeting, thx!"

It's moments like this, when you are extremely grateful to have contacts like Stacey in your internal network. But it also demonstrates, how important it is to build such networks, and how you can rely upon them when least expected. As a PA you never know what you will be tasked with next!

The personal assistant directory

Does a document or file exist within your organisation detailing which PA supports which manager – a PA directory? Does the directory include full contact details of global PAs across the business, or is it limited to the PAs in your country or your site location? If such information isn't readily available, seek it out.

If there isn't a directory of PAs across the business, create one. If you are a junior PA and recognise that there is a requirement for such a list, approach a senior PA at your organisation and ask for his/her approval before you embark upon your task. Remember, that this responsibility may already sit with someone else, so make your enquiries first. Offer to take ownership of maintaining the PA directory once it's established. Include your name at the bottom of the directory together with your contact details. By doing so, you are making yourself visible to your global PA colleagues.

 Use the template overleaf, and create a PA directory for your company or your country (depending on the size of your organisation).

Once you have either sourced, or created, an internal directory of PAs within your business, ensure it's accessible to others. If you have a company intranet, approach the manager of the site and request that your document is uploaded, for employees to access. If reference documents such as organisation charts, are held in a centrally shared folder on the company network, upload your PA directory to that folder. Does your company have an internal desktop messaging system or a virtual noticeboard? Again, publish your document for others to view.

The more you promote awareness of your PA colleagues throughout the organisation, the better. For instance, if all managers across the business are aware of which PA manages which executive's diary, they will more than likely contact the PA directly, when they are seeking diary time in the executive's diary. This is a faster route for the requestor, who can obtain a quick response from the PA as diary manager. Increasing the awareness of PAs across the business, will also reinforce the PA network and elevate the support services which you provide.

Add to bible...

Add the PA directory to your bible for easy reference. Also email it directly to your PA colleagues.

Use the contact information from the new PA directory to establish an Outlook distribution group for all of the PAs within your organisation.

Global Directory of Personal Assistants at Bayleys Global Finance Management

Country	Subsidiary Name	PA	Executive	Time Zone of PA	Email Address	International tel. no.
UK	Bayleys UK	Gemma Rafferty	Peter Simons, CEO UK	GMT	gemma.rafferty@bayleys.com	00 44 xxxx xxxxxx
UK	Bayleys UK	Kate Buckeridge	Chris McCarthy, CFO UK	GMT	kate.buckeridge@bayleys.com	00 44 xxxx xxxxxx
USA	Bayleys Group	Whitney Novak	Liam Hess, Chairman	EDT	whitney.novak@bayleys.com	00 1 xxxx xxxxxx
USA	Bayleys Group	Kristin Edwards	Howard Stem, CEO US	EDT	kristin.edwards@bayleys.com	00 1 xxxx xxxxxx
France	Bayleys France	Nadine Chevalier	Olivier Durand, EVP Operations	CET	nadine.chevalier@bayleys.com	00 33 xxxx xxxxxx
France	Bayleys France	Bernadette Garcia	Louis Rousseau, Head of Financial Management	CET	bernadette.garcia@bayleys.com	00 33 xxxx xxxxxx
Germany	Bayleys Germany	Anna Schneider	Klaus Wagner, Head of Corporate Tax	CET	anna.schneider@bayleys.com	00 49 xxxx xxxxxx
Germany	Bayleys Germany	Katja Schwarz	Stefan Jung, Financial Audit Manager	CET	katja.schwarz@bayleys.com	00 49 xxxx xxxxxx

For any amends please contact
Gemma.Rafferty@bayleys.com

Adapt the template to suit your company structure e.g. list by town or city locations, add direct dial details, mobile numbers, or site addresses.

If you are employed by a large company who employs several PAs across the business, consider establishing a private networking group on LinkedIn for the PAs. This works especially well for international companies, as a tool to unite PAs who would not normally meet.

Use the newly formed community to exchange information on company processes, request local information from your international peers e.g. local hotel rates and transfer times, and share information about your own local site. If you are the owner of your company's PA LinkedIn group, the responsibility is yours to monitor posts, promote awareness of the group and assess requests from new members to join. It's a great way of communicating and bringing your PA colleagues together, virtually, if this cannot be achieved face to face.

External business networking

When you have established your internal network within your organisation, consider your external network. Building a network with your external company contacts is just as important as the internal contacts you will continue to build, within your immediate office environment. For example, your business executive has regular meetings with the Operational Director at FedEx. The FedEx account is worth £300K per annum to your company. Build your rapport with the Operational Director's PA at FedEx, so when your executive asks you to cancel a meeting at short notice, it's not a problem. Your existing relationship with the Operational Director's PA, will smooth the way for a potentially damaging request to reschedule a diary appointment, which was agreed 2 months ago. If you find yourself in this situation, but aren't aware who is your point of contact at the external company, ask someone in your organisation's internal network. A fellow PA in your company should have the details.

TOP TIPS

Whenever you make a new external PA contact who you know will be a valuable link e.g. PA to EVP Sales FedEx, save the contact details to your Outlook contacts. List the company name and full name and job title of the executive the PA supports. Add the date to the notes for future reference, so at a glance it's obvious when you last spoke, and how current the information is on your contacts card.

Networking also offers fantastic opportunities for supplier research, and insights. If you have been asked to organise a corporate event, and are considering venues, ask the appropriate people in your network for their personal recommendations. Which venue have they used for a corporate event recently and would they recommend it? Which venues would they definitely avoid? What was the feedback from their guests? Were the venue staff efficient and courteous? Was it value for money? This is invaluable information which cannot be found on the internet, and will enable you to make an informed and educated decision on venue hire. Asking others in your network about venues, could also provide you with an alternative venue location, which you hadn't considered.

I was recently asked to find an offsite meeting venue in central London at short notice, for an executive meeting. My brief was to source a meeting room between 1430 and 1700, on the Wednesday afternoon, for 5 attendees, at a hotel venue in Mayfair. Mayfair is one of the most expensive locations in London, and therefore room hire fees were top of mind when completing my brief. However, my workload dictated that I could not spend hours sourcing a venue and negotiating rates. The time at my disposal, for this task, was approximately 30 minutes. As time was so limited, I decided to consult a networking group for inside information.

The PA Club in London is an established networking group, and in addition to an online venue directory, the group offers a dedicated advisory service 'Ask Abbie'. I did exactly that, and the PA Club's 'Abbie' promptly provided me with contact details for the events managers at 2 hotels in Mayfair – Flemings and the Athenaeum. I emailed my brief to both meeting and events managers, and asked them to provide a quote. Within 30 minutes both had responded with their rates. The Athenaeum provided me with the most competitive rate, and after further negotiations on the price, I secured another price reduction and confirmed the booking with them. Mayfair hotels commonly charge £500 for half a day meeting room hire, and I had secured a meeting room at a 5 star, luxury hotel at £350 including VAT. Ultimately, this result had been achieved so quickly by approaching the PA Club for venue referrals. This is a great example of how networking groups can be a valuable resource, when seeking information, contacts and referrals.

Meeting suppliers

If you are looking for a new supplier, view the online directory on your PA networking group website, for referrals. Remember that the information exchange is two way, so if you have a supplier who you'd like to recommend – contact the network owner with the supplier details. Advise your supplier, who will no doubt be pleased with your referral.

PA networking groups also facilitate 'meet the supplier' events. For instance, the Aberdeen PA network, in Scotland, co-ordinates supplier showcase events, where approximately 100 local suppliers are invited to exhibit their products and services, for an invited audience of local PAs. This allows local suppliers to promote their business to PAs who are normally office based from 9-5, and whom they would never meet. Attendees can also provide feedback to suppliers regarding what they are looking for as a PA, and where gaps exist in the market place. If your local networking group hosts a 'meet the suppliers' event – give it a go. They are fun and sociable events, with suppliers offering free samples and advice. Grab yourself a glass of wine and get networking. Meet the supplier events often include a raffle or competition, where you could be fortunate enough to win a free hotel stay for 2, a day at the local spa hotel, or a flower bouquet or corporate gift.

Add to bible…

Following your attendance at a 'meet the suppliers' event, note down the suppliers details which are of interest in your bible, for easy reference. Next time you are seeking a corporate gift or alternative venue, you can peruse your bible for inspiration and will have a direct contact for that company.

Career opportunities

Networking is also a valuable tool, when you are seeking a new career opportunity. You may discover your ideal job by networking across different channels e.g. online networking sites, LinkedIn, your local PA networking group, or your professional association. Furthermore, consider approaching your family and friends network, for word of mouth opportunities. Your next job lead could come from anywhere. Don't discount the people you meet in the elevator, the bar of the hotel you are staying at, the driver of your cab, the lady sat next to you on your regular train journey to work. Treat all network opportunities as informal job searches, if you are in the market place. You never know where it may lead.

Approximately 90% of employers use some form of social media for their recruitment process, and evidence demonstrates that they achieve successful results. Global trends indicate that companies are most likely to use LinkedIn, Facebook and Twitter for direct online recruitment and candidate research. Recruitment agencies also follow this trend, by using online networking sites for candidate search and selection.

Without a doubt, the most powerful online business networking resource is LinkedIn. Companies with in-house recruiters use LinkedIn as their shop front for advertising vacancies, and reach out to individuals on LinkedIn who could potentially be the correct fit for a particular role (headhunting). LinkedIn allows recruiters to connect with both passive and active candidates to discuss job opportunities. Recruitment consultants and executive search specialists post vacancies online, review candidate's profiles and evaluate their career history.

 If you are seeking a new PA position, use LinkedIn as your online career networking resource and kick start your search. All job hunting activity on LinkedIn is private, so you can search in confidence.

LinkedIn allows users to search for vacancies, view jobs, save searches (so you are notified automatically of new opportunities), post your CV, receive and give peer endorsements, build your profile, and add your experience to attract attention from recruiters and employers.

If you are considering relocating, there is the facility within LinkedIn to search for jobs by country and by city. You can also search and follow the companies where you are seeking employment.

Create or refresh your LinkedIn profile. Then read it from a recruiter's perspective. What does it say to recruiters? Is your profile professional, positive and marketable? Are you selling your skills and experience as much as you possibly can? Be confident when writing your profile, it's your chance to get noticed. When your profile is finalised, ask a friend to review it for you.

Update your LinkedIn profile if you have been made redundant, or your temporary post has come to an end, to reflect that you are actively seeking a new position.

Job opportunities can also present themselves, via your regional PA networking group. To hear about such vacancies complete some informal networking, and ask members of the group if their employer is currently recruiting, and if they are aware of any openings. If your search is targeted towards a particular sector or company, approach a networking contact who is already employed in that sector or company, and convey your interest in any future opportunities. If your search is at its formative stage, complete some general recruitment research. Ask members of your network group 'how regularly does your employer recruit back office staff?', 'where does your employer advertise new vacancies?', or 'which local recruitment agency would you recommend?'

If you are a student or junior PA looking for an opening into a company, this approach could be particularly effective. For instance, if you're just starting out, your CV may be discounted by a recruiter, due to lack of experience. However, if your personality, professionalism and motivation is recognised at a networking group, it could open doors to job offers for you.

Recruitment consultants often approach networking groups directly to promote job opportunities, and tap into their target market of PAs. Build your rapport with local agencies via your networking group, so when you decide the time is right for a career move, you have already established a personal contact with the relevant consultant. Keep yourself 'top of mind' with the individuals who are close to the vacancies, and who can aid you with your career search. If you are actively seeking a career move - ramp up your networking activities!

Actively connect with people via LinkedIn. Make an effort to do this regularly and continue to grow your network on a daily basis.

If you are an experienced business networker, have raised your profile by attending various face to face networking events, and contributed to online networking forums, you may experience head-hunters approaching you directly with job opportunities. Congratulations! All that networking has escalated your profile to the level that recruiters are seeking you out!

Prior to publishing this book, I have been regularly approached by head hunters via LinkedIn, who have asked me to consider some fantastic PA opportunities. The companies who have approached me include HSBC, Super Dry, Clarks Shoes, Royal Mail, Dyson, Wargaming.net, House of Fraser and Amazon. These are seriously impressive companies, and although the opportunities weren't right for me at the time, I was immensely proud to have attracted their interest via LinkedIn. It demonstrates that a well written LinkedIn profile, together with the relevant experience, will attract a recruiter's attention. Below is copy of a an original email, I received earlier this year:

Opportunity at Clarks – "I'd love to talk to you"

Dear Maria,

I am currently looking for an exceptional EA to support our Chief Brand Office (Global Brand Director) at Clarks and on seeing your profile wanted to reach out to see if this would be of interest to you.

The Brand Director is relatively new to Clarks and his career within the Marketing and Brand world is amazing, having worked at Ralph Lauren, Alexander McQueen and Nike, and he is looking for a superstar to support him as an EA. He is keen to recruit someone who has a keen interest in Marketing and would like to develop a career in this space in the future.

Would you be interested in having a chat with me about this fantastic opportunity?

Kind Regards

Katherine Drew
Resourcing Manager, Clarks

A recruiter advised me recently that when searching for a suitable EA for his client, he cross checked candidate's LinkedIn profiles against the CVs he had received. He was amazed by how many poor LinkedIn profiles there were. Some applicants had not spent time on their Linkedin profile, information was missing or contained errors and some profiles were just plain shoddy. My contact believes a LinkedIn profile is your online CV, and as a result he downgraded those with the poor profiles, and they weren't selected for interview.

Take a look at my Linkedin profile as an example of the material you can include. Consider what work examples you can upload, who could provide you with recommendations and which skills you can add.

UK PA networking groups

PA networking groups supplement the information and resources you can source, through your professional association. Groups act as an 'information exchange' for you and your peers. They provide a portal, for you to connect with fellow PAs who share a mutual interest in your chosen sector, and to connect you with PAs working in your geographic location. There is also a fun and social element to networking events. You could make lifelong friends and contacts, it's not all about business! As there isn't a membership fee involved, you can join multiple networking groups, and attend events which suit your personal calendar. If you are working in a different location to normal, the opportunity is there to connect with that arEAs regional group, and make new friends in that location.

Search online for a PA networking group in your region. For a current list of PA networks that exist in the UK visit **www.pa-assist.com/networks**. At the time of writing, the networking groups in existence in the UK (with free membership) are:

UK PA Networking Groups	Website
Aberdeen PA Network	scottishpanetwork.com
Belfast PA Network	twitter.com/belfastpas
Berkshire & North Hampshire PA Network	twitter.com/BNHPANetwork
Bristol PA Network	bristolpanetwork.co.uk
Buckinghamshire PA Network	buckspanetwork.co.uk
Cardiff PA Network	cardiffpanetwork.com
Exeter PA Network	exeterpanetwork.com
Glasgow PA	scottishpanetwork.com
Guernsey PA Connect	guernseypaconnect.com
Hull & Humber, Yorks	panetwork.co.uk
Leeds and York - The PA Hub	thepahub.co.uk
London PA Network	london-pa-network.org
London City Airport Premier PA club	Londoncityairport.com (under corporate tab)
Manchester PA Network	manchesterpanetwork.co.uk
Mid Sussex PA/EA Networking	twitter.com/midsussexpas
Newcastle PA Network	newcastlepanetwork.com
Norwich PA Network	twitter.com/PANorwich
Oxford PA Network	oxfordpanetwork.co.uk
Oxfordshire PA Club	ox-pa.com
The PA Club (London)	thepaclub.com
Peterborough PAs	twitter.com/PboroPA
Plymouth PA Network	plymouthpanetwork.co.uk
Society of Virtual Assistants	societyofvirtualassistants.co.uk
Wales NHS PA Network	twitter.com/NHSPAsWales

PA networking groups often facilitate mentoring partnerships, which is a very useful mechanism for those starting out, and wishing to develop or progress their career paths. Mentoring partnerships unite two personal assistants (one senior and one junior), who have both committed to the scheme. The senior PA acts as mentor to the junior PA (the mentee), providing encouragement and professional advice. The junior PA benefits from the insights, guidance and professional advice.

 Ask your regional PA networking group about mentoring partnerships. If you are an experienced PA and would like to support a junior PA in the business, consider offering your services as 'Mentor'. If you think you could benefit from a senior PAs insights and deeper knowledge, enquire about 'Mentee' opportunities.

Global PA networking groups

Online PA networking groups exist all over the world – thanks to LinkedIn. Here is a snap shot of groups in existence, together with total membership numbers, to demonstrate the popularity of PA networking around the world. All groups can be found on LinkedIn.

Global PA Networking Groups (LinkedIn)	No. of Members
Administrative Assistant	156,325
Executive/Personal Assistants	151,572
Personal Assistant and Office Manager (PAOM)	110,242
Global Executive Assistants	99,201
PAs, Eas, Vas and senior Administrators	76,403
Executive Assistants to CEOs	69,063
International Association of Administrative Professionals (IAAP)	42,655
e-LEGAL Support: Legal Secretary, Paralegals, Virtual Assistants, Law Clerks & Admin Staff	36,313
Executive Assistant / Secretary	33,742

The Effective Admin – Administrative Assistant and Executive Assistant Group	**32,424**
Virtual Assistant Start-Ups	**28,629**
American Society of Administrative Professionals (ASAP)	**19,697**
EA PA AUSTRALIA & NZ	**4,175**
Executive Assistants Org - Silicon Valley	**3,810**
Dubai PA Club	**1,864**
Australian EAs PAs Secretaries Office Managers Administrators Group	**1,553**
Secretary.it - Manager Assistant Network	**1,454**

If there isn't a networking group in your location, consider establishing one. For inspiration, review an existing group's website for ideas of networking events or web design. If you are fortunate to find such a network in your area, join the community and you'll reap the rewards for years to come. Remember that these networking groups are FREE to join.

Do you support a Global CEO, Country Head or EVP of Business Development who travels frequently to a foreign city on business? Consider connecting with a PA network in that city, even if you aren't based there.

By connecting with a networking group in that City, you can tap into local knowledge regarding hotels, venues, drivers, restaurants and view their supplier directory online for referrals and ideas. Explain to the network owner why you wish to connect, and that your manager frequently spends time in that city. When your research is complete, impress your manager with your local knowledge of where is best to eat out, details of the local tram or shuttle service, and recommend a new hotel which is getting great reviews. Your executive will be amazed that you have gone the extra mile and sourced such detail, in such an innovative way.

Attending your first networking event

The natural progression from joining an online networking group, is to attend a local networking event. This is your opportunity to meet other PAs face to face, meet suppliers and make new friends. Once you have practised your online networking, and networking with friends, family and colleagues, it's time to move up a gear and head into the professional arena of a business networking event. If you've tried some of the various networking channels explained in this chapter, you will already have experienced the benefits of networking as a personal assistant. If the idea of attending such an event, fills you with dread, treat it as a learning curve. Do your research online as to what's available nearby.

Choose an event which has another interesting focus e.g. a supplier showcase, an award winning PA providing a presentation, or an industry expert sharing their business insights. Where is the event being hosted? If it's a venue you're not familiar with perhaps the event incorporates a show around of the facilities, meeting rooms and restaurant. If the event is being hosted by a city hotel, the hotel will inevitably market themselves to the PAs attending, in order to promote their services and secure new business. What could be nicer than a hotel show around, complimentary drinks and nibbles at a 5 star establishment, watching an industry expert presentation, and making new PA friends? Go on, what is there to be afraid of?

Ensure you have completed your preparation prior to attending your first networking event, it will make it easier, you will feel confident and focused and the rewards will be greater. Read the published Agenda thoroughly. Who is hosting? Who is speaking? Google those individuals and complete your research on their background, memorise their names, review their LinkedIn profiles. If this is a networking group which is hosted on LinkedIn, view the member's area of that group. Scroll down to see who could be attending. Is there anyone in particular you should seek out, or could benefit from connecting with? Work through the tips which follow, prior to attending your first networking event.

Describe yourself – the elevator pitch
If you were to meet a potentially important contact for the first time in an elevator, at a conference, and they ask you: "What do you do?" you have no more than 20 seconds, perhaps just 10-15 seconds, between floors to explain, and to make such an impressive impact that the person asks for your contact details. This is what's known as the **elevator pitch** and the principle translates to meeting anyone for the first time, when they ask you 'What do you do?' Your pitch should include your name, company name or sector, job title, location, and a summary of what you do and your experience. Keep it simple to understand, and not overly technical. Don't baffle people with terminology they don't understand. Your elevator pitch should also be engaging, interesting and concise. Prepare your elevator pitch and have 2 versions ready. A 20 second version for the quick introduction and a lengthier 'part 2' version for when you have more time, and when it feels appropriate to go into more detail. Rehearse your pitch so you know it from memory.

Version 1

"Hi, my name is Gemma Rafferty, I work at Bayleys Global Financial Management as the PA to the CEO. I've supported the CEO for the last 2 years and been with the company for 5. I love my job and I live in Islington, London".

Version 2

"Hi, my name is Gemma Rafferty, I work for Bayleys Global Financial Management as the PA to the CEO. I manage Board meetings, look after executive diaries, manage global travel and co-ordinate events. It's a demanding job but I love it. I've supported our CEO for 2 years, been with the company for 5. My experience spans the last 10 years, mostly in financial services and I really enjoy event management. I live in Islington, London".

Add to bible… Create your own elevator pitch and add to your bible. Memorise it, update it when necessary, repeat it and say it out loud with confidence.

Take a problem with you

Before you head to your PA networking event, spend a few minutes thinking about what you want to learn from others. Networking is about giving and receiving advice, so think about what you need help with. Having identified your current work headaches, formulate a few questions to ask at the event such as "I'm seeking a new airport transfer company for senior managers, my current supplier is retiring, could you recommend anyone?" or "My manager has requested I organise gifts for the Board Members at Christmas, I have no idea what to purchase, what would you recommend?" or "Our global CEO, who is French, is visiting our regional office next month and has specific catering requirements. Could you recommend a private wine merchant who delivers locally?"

The onus is upon delegates to give support and share information. Having interesting and unique questions to ask at the event, will engage your fellow PAs, provide interest, make a memorable impression and potentially unearth the solution to your problem. Finally, observe these quick tips when attending your first PA networking event.

Quick Tips

- Dress the part – dress smartly, appearance is important
- Smile and be confident
- Be approachable
- Take business cards with you
- Don't be a wall flower – be brave and introduce yourself
- Adapt to your audience
- Aim to connect with 4 people – quality is better than quantity
- Inject some humour into your conversations – make people smile
- Ask open questions, keep the conversation flowing
- Be aware of your body language
- Be courteous and polite
- Be positive – never moan about your manager or company
- Don't talk about the weather, it's boring and unimaginative

- Ask people about themselves – what industry do you work in? Is this your first networking event? Do you know many people here tonight? Do you live locally? How did you start out as a PA?
- Above all, relax, be sociable and have some fun!

Post the PA network event, you will have numerous business cards in your pocket. Follow up ASAP by connecting with each individual via LinkedIn. Send a personal message with your connection request, reminding them of where you met and save their contact details in your Outlook contacts. Add a note to their Outlook contact card of the date and event where you met.

8

An Introduction to Business Travel

What's in this chapter?

Most business executives are required to travel considerable distances for meetings with colleagues, prospects, clients and suppliers. Whilst modern technology is available to provide cheaper alternatives, such as video conferencing, audio conferencing and online meetings, the importance of face to face meetings remains paramount. Long lasting relationships can be effectively established and nurtured (with the face to face approach), which would be difficult to sustain with a remote relationship. Business travel is particularly essential for business development executives. Very few sales are secured without a direct pitch, a product demonstration or a face to face meeting with the client. In this chapter we will discover:

* Where does your manager travel
* Your local transport infrastructure
* Your hub airport
* UK airports
* London airports explained
* Classes of air travel
* Business travel acronyms
* Wi-Fi for the business traveller
* Business travel news
* Alternatives to business travel

For all businesses, the need to meet clients, customers and suppliers, will involve travelling to see them at some point in time. These 'business travellers' will be key to the company they work for, and it's often a PAs duty and responsibility to ensure that their corporate travel is managed as effectively as possible, with the best routes flown, the least lay over time possible, and the best fares secured. Booking business travel can take up to 50% of your day (if you're supporting a senior level executive), so having a greater depth of knowledge in this area will be a huge asset. Business travel is not only complex, it's also expensive, and mistakes made in this area could have huge ramifications for you and your executive. Work through the different elements in this chapter, and you'll have a good start to understanding business travel, and greater awareness of all the factors to consider, when co-ordinating your executive's next trip.

Where does your manager travel?

Due to many organisations having a global presence, it's highly probable that your manager regularly uses air transport to travel to meetings. This could be a domestic flight, or international, or a combination of both. To assist your business traveller to maximise their meeting time, and minimise their travel time, it's important to understand their regular travel requirements. Completing initial research into your manager's travel habits, will provide you with an overview of their travel. If you are new to your position you may be fortunate enough to receive handover training, and business travel will be one of the key points covered. However, if a handover hasn't been an option, approach your manager, advise that you are collating data around his/her business travel, and ask about the common routes travelled and destinations.

 It's imperative you understand your exec's travelling habits, routes flown, preferred hotels, favourite airline, frequent flyer numbers, locations visited. Book a meeting with your exec to discuss 'business travel' and ask the relevant questions.

Use the sample questions below, to obtain key travel information from your exec:

* Where do you travel on business?
* Is this an internal or external company location?
* Is this an inner city or a suburban area?
* What duration do you usually stay for?
* How frequently do you travel there?
* Which means of transport do you use e.g. rail, air or self-drive?

An introduction to business travel

- When flying which airline is preferred?
- Do you hold any frequent flyer memberships?
- Which is your preferred hotel chain?

Create a regular travel dashboard, detailing the basics of your manager's most frequent trips. Use the template below as a guide. The examples provided are for a UK business traveller, who uses London Heathrow as their outbound airport. The dashboard will be your quick reference guide, for future trip co-ordination.

REGULAR TRAVEL DASHBOARD

NEW YORK
Area: Downtown Manhattan
Trip Duration: 4 days
Transport: Air
Operator: British Airways, Virgin Atlantic
Airport: LHR-JFK or LGA
Preferred Hotel: Westin, Times Square

MIAMI
Area: Miami Beach
Trip Duration: 5 days
Transport: Air
Operator: British Airways, Virgin Atlantic, American Airlines
Airport: LHR-MIA
Preferred Hotel: Loews Miami Beach

CAPE TOWN
Area: Cape Town City Centre
Trip Duration: 5 days
Transport: Air
Operator: British Airways, Virgin Atlantic
Airport: LHR-CPT
Preferred Hotel: Table Bay Hotel

NEW DELHI
Area: Gurgaon
Trip Duration: 4 days
Transport: Air
Operator: British Airways, Air India, Virgin Atlantic
Airport: LHR-DEL
Preferred Hotel: The Oberoi

LONDON
Area: Square Mile
Trip Duration: 2 days
Transport: Overland Rail
Operator: South West Trains
Airport: n/a
Preferred Hotel: The Grange

GLASGOW
Area: Glasgow City Centre
Trip Duration: 2 days
Transport: Air
Operator: British Airways
Airport: LHR-GLA
Preferred Hotel: Blythswood Hotel

You can continue to build your travel dashboard, as you book new trips for your executive. Did you know, that business execs who fly in excess of 40 flights per annum are referred to as **road warriors**?

Your local transport infrastructure

It's vital to research your own local transport infrastructure, to understand the means of transport available to visiting business executives, and for executives departing from your office location travelling further afield. Without understanding your local infrastructure, you will struggle to provide the best transport options for your executive. Your local infrastructure will include public transport options, but the most common means of transport utilised for business travel are:

- Road (self-drive own vehicle, car rental, chauffer driven vehicle, taxi)
- Rail (overland rail, underground rail, Eurostar)
- Air (charter flight, private jet charter, helicopter)

An introduction to business travel

If you are new to an organisation, your manager will no doubt advise you of the existing transport links available, and which airport is closest to your office, but do your own research to check this information is accurate. You may discover a new route, a new airline carrier, or a travel alternative which your manager was unaware of. Airline operators do not always effectively communicate changes to routes, especially if they are discontinuing a route, so make your own investigations to ensure you have current information. To begin with, start with your office location. Which airport is the closest? Is there an alternative airport nearby which has been dismissed previously? Research the points below:

* What is the distance from your office to the local airport?
* What transport links are available between the 2?
* What is the travel time for the different means of transport?
* Is there an airport hotel suitable for business travellers?
* Which airline carriers are operating?
* Are low cost airlines in operation?
* Does it operate domestic and international flights?

The airport closest to your office location will be known as your **local airport**.

 Talk to your PA peers at your office location, to gain a further understanding of local travel options, which taxi company is preferred, and which is the closest mainline rail station.

Next, consider your executive's location. What is their home address? Which airport is closest to their address? It may not be the airport which you've identified as being your **local airport**, it all depends on where your executive lives. For example, your company's head office is in Bristol, but your manager resides in Oxford. The closest airport to your office is Bristol International Airport, however the closest airport to your manager's home address is London Heathrow. Therefore, you should research London Heathrow in addition to your local airport. The airport which you frequently book travel to and from, for your executive, will be known as your **hub airport**. Complete the same research for the **hub airport** as you did for your local airport, but use your executive's home address as the starting point.

Add to bible...   When you've completed the research on both your local and hub airports, add the data into your bible. Keep the information concise, and use bullet points for quick reference.

Your hub airport

Now that you've identified your executive's hub airport, and have completed some basic research into the transport links, it's very important to complete a familiarisation trip to that airport. You can gain a wealth of information from an airport's website, but nothing will match the experience of travelling to that airport, standing in the check-in area, and understanding how your executive travels through the terminal. By attending in person and viewing the airport, you will vastly increase your knowledge, discover facilities which you didn't know existed, and appreciate the scale of the terminal building. You will also have a better understanding of the parking facilities available, the transport links to different terminals, and the location of the airport lounges and on site restaurants. Visiting your hub airport will help you with travel timings in future, as you've experienced the layout first hand.

 Plan a visit to your hub airport. Request a tour from the airport marketing team, and explain that you are a frequent business travel booker. Familiarise yourself with the airport layout, distance between gates and terminals, parking services and ground transportation services.

 London City Airport provides **behind the scenes** tours for PAs, which are free of charge.
Email: PremierPA@londoncityairport.com for further details.

If there are several PAs in your office which are co-ordinating business travel from the same hub airport, see if you can organise a group visit to that airport.

Establish a personal relationship with your hub airport's marketing or business development team. Is there a forum you could join to provide feedback on, on behalf of your business travellers within your company? Become your company's representative for business travellers at your hub airport.

Use the familiarisation checklist over, when visiting your hub airport.

Airport Familiarisation Checklist

Transfer to/from the Airport
- ☐ Driving distance/duration
- ☐ Drop off area for taxi and private drivers
- ☐ Is there a dedicated taxi company at the airport
- ☐ Overland rail connections to airport
- ☐ Underground rail connections to airport
- ☐ Car parking: what is available e.g. short stay, long stay, pre-booking, online reservations, valet parking, fees
- ☐ Travel from car park to terminal (bus/pod) time required
- ☐ Hotel shuttle services available
- ☐ Recommended chauffeur or limo provider

The Airport
- ☐ Check-in options
  - o Fast track security
  - o Bag drop area
  - o Self-service check in
- ☐ Where can private drivers 'meet & greet' travellers on arrival
- ☐ Business lounges
  - o Lounge options available
  - o Compatibility with your execs airline alliance
  - o Additional fees
  - o Terminal locations
- ☐ Number of terminals, terminal maps
- ☐ Outbound destinations from terminals
- ☐ Travel distance and type between terminals (mono rail, shuttle)
- ☐ Amenities for the business traveller
  - o Wi-Fi connectivity
  - o Showers
  - o Business centre
- ☐ What is the IATA airport code

Airport Communications
- ☐ Airport app
- ☐ E-newsletter
- ☐ Frequent traveller loyalty or reward scheme
- ☐ Business traveller forum
- ☐ Twitter, Facebook
- ☐ PA club

UK airports

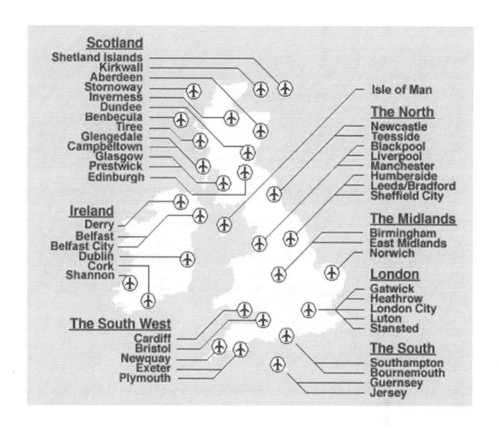

Find out if your local airport has a PA networking group which you could join. London City Airport has its own **Premier PA Club** for PAs, EAs and Office Managers, who book business travel. Members receive regular newsletters, useful tips, invitations to exclusive events, competitions and behind the scenes tours of the airport.

London airports explained

London has 5 major airports: London City, London Heathrow, London Gatwick, London Luton and London Stansted. Depending on the route flown, preferred carrier and meeting destination, it's worth considering the different airports, but be aware of the travel times to central London - if you choose an airport in greater London e.g. Gatwick, Luton or Stanstead. Flying into one of those airports, may incur an additional 60 minutes travel time for your business traveller. If your executive is heading into London from Europe, you may find London City your best choice (it's the closest to central London), if your road warrior is travelling in from Salt Lake City on business, then London Heathrow could be the best fit (with many direct, long haul, options).

London City Airport (LCY)	City = 7 miles
LCY is the only London airport situated in London itself, just 3 miles from Canary Wharf, 7 miles from the City and 10 miles from London's West End, linked to the underground via Docklands Light Railway. Flights to London City Airport are generally booked by business people, looking to gain quick and easy access to the financial districts of Canary Wharf and the Square Mile. Also home to London City Airport's Private Jet Centre, which means HNWI's arrive closer to the key business districts.	
To/from the airport: Docklands light railway provides a direct service to Bank tube station in the square mile (22 mins). Taxi, or chauffeur.	
London Heathrow Airport (LHR)	City = 18 miles
LHR is 18 miles west of central London. The largest airport in the UK and the 3rd busiest in the world. Heathrow is London's long haul hub and is the most popular arrival point for flights from the United States. A sprawling airport with 5 terminals, so allow for travel time through the airport and airport approach. Various hotels are located close by the numerous airport terminals.	
To/from the airport: the Heathrow Express train is the fastest route to central London and connects with Paddington Station in west London (20 mins). LHR is also connected to the London underground Piccadilly line – allow 60 mins journey time for central London. Taxis/chauffeur options are available, but can be an expensive option and take longer.	

London Gatwick Airport (LGW)	City = 28 miles
LGW is located 28 miles south of London. London Gatwick Airport is the second-busiest international airport in the UK after Heathrow (in terms of passenger traffic), despite its considerable distance from central London. Gatwick flies to more destinations than any other UK Airport. EasyJet is Gatwick's largest customer, they fly 41% of the total number of passengers at the airport. Hotels available within walking distance to terminals.	
To/from the airport: the Gatwick Express trains run every 15 minutes and the journey time is approx. 30 minutes to London Victoria. Travelling by road to central London is approximately 60-70 minutes, and will cost a considerable amount by taxi.	
London Luton Airport (LTN)	City = 35 miles
LTN is located 35 miles northeast of London. Flights to London Luton Airport are mainly offered by low-cost carriers (budget airlines) which operate in Europe. However, travellers should consider the inconvenience of an airport location which is a considerable distance from central London.	
To/from the airport: A shuttle bus links Luton Airport with Luton Airport Parkway Station, from where there are regular trains to Blackfriars, City Thameslink, Farringdon and St Pancras International. Average 40 mins train journey plus 10 mins shuttle bus to airport. Taxi and chauffeur options available.	
London Stansted Airport (STN)	City = 38 miles
STN is located 38 miles northeast of central London. It's the 4th busiest UK airport. Stansted Airport is a hub for a number of major European low cost carriers. Stansted's runway is also used by private companies such as the Harrods Aviation terminal which is opposite the main terminal building, and handles private jets and some state visits.	
To/from the airport: Stansted Express rail service runs from the airport train station, which is only 2 mins walk from the airport terminal, towards Liverpool Street station, in the financial district (journey time 47 mins). Taxi and chauffeur options available.	

London City Airport
Get closer.

- Best London airport for flight punctuality
- Only 20 mins from terminal entrance to departure lounge
- On arrival, just 15 mins from plane to train

  - 14 mins to Canary Wharf
  - 22 mins to Bank
  - 25 mins to Westminster

Fast, punctual and actually in London.

For timetables or to book flights visit:
londoncityairport.com

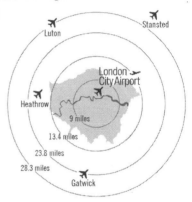

Does your executive regularly use a London airport? Have you considered another London airport as an alternative? Next time, you are booking flights to or from London, consider London City Airport. It's the only airport in central London – and transport links to the city area are good. Often overlooked as LHR is dominant – you may be surprised by the routes flown, and your boss will appreciate the quick transfer time through the airport terminal.

Sign up for your hub airport's communications to keep abreast of news, new routes flown, offers and changes of timetables. Communications available will be across various media e.g. e-newsletters, Twitter and Facebook. Is there an airport App? Download it and familiarise yourself with the functions available.

Classes of air travel

Airlines traditionally have 3 travel classes 'First', 'Business' and 'Economy'. Some carriers operate an additional 4th option on long haul flights; this is called 'Premium Economy'.

First class

First-class travel is the most expensive but offers the most comfort and amenities. First class affords the largest legroom (seat pitch), largest seat width, fine dining, complimentary alcohol and premium service. Seats (or cabins), are located in the front of the aircraft which are notable for their space, comfort, service and privacy. First class fares are often out of policy for corporate business travellers.

Business class

Business class is tailored for the needs of frequent business travellers. It is mid-priced between First and Economy. This class provides a larger seat pitch than economy with improved seat width and comfort. The exact name for business class may vary by operator e.g. Virgin Atlantic brand theirs 'Upper class'.

Premium economy class

Available on some long haul flights, this class is a tier up from economy with increased seat width and leg room. If your travel policy doesn't allow Business Class travel, Premium Economy can be a great choice. You'll have upgraded seats and an Economy ticket on your expense report.

Economy class

Entry level class (fondly referred to as cattle class in the industry). The cheapest seat options available with minimal seat width, minimal leg room and basic meal options. Economy travel provides the price conscious traveller with a cheaper alternative, but with a compromise on comfort. Also referred to as 'Standard' or 'Coach'. For business executives 'economy' is often standard for short haul, but consider upgrading for long haul flights.

Whilst 'First', 'Business' and 'Economy' are standard names of travel classes, several operators use their own alternative, branded names. For example British Airways use the following terms:

First	First - selected international flights
Business	Club Europe - flights within Europe Club World - longer international flights Club World London City - between London City and New York JFK
Premium Economy	World Traveller Plus - selected international flights
Economy	UK Domestic - flights within the UK Euro Traveller - flights within Europe World Traveller - longer international flights

Familiarise yourself with your executive's preferred airline operator. Which terms do they use to describe their Economy, Business and First class fares?

Check your company's travel policy for guidance on which travel class is permitted. The difference in price can be huge, especially for long haul, so ensure you are following protocol before selecting a business or first fare class.

View the aircraft image over. Note the size and spacing of the seats in First class, then view the bottom of the image for the Economy seats (World Traveller). See how compacted it is in Economy. View the layout of Business (Club World) see how the seats are placed at opposites.

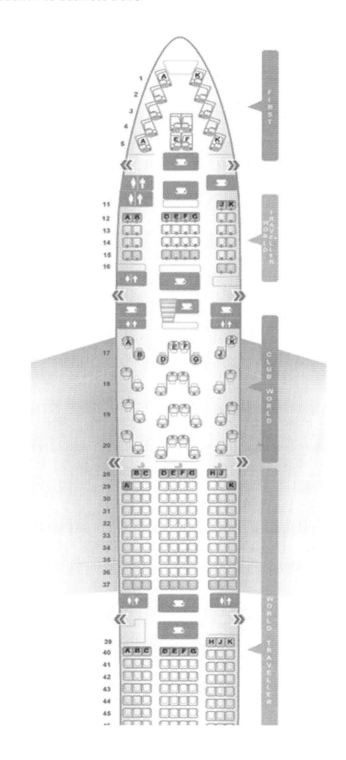

Business travel acronyms

There are numerous acronyms and abbreviations in use, within the business travel and travel management industries. Familiarise yourself with the list below to avoid confusion, and increase your understanding of industry terms.

ADR	Average Daily Rate
APIS	Advanced Passenger Information System
B&B	Bed and Breakfast
BAR	Best Available Rate
BTA	Business Travel Agent
BTC	Business Travel Centre
CRO	Central Reservation Office
CRS	Central Reservation System
CTA	Close to Arrival
DDR	Day Delegate Rate
FFP	Frequent Flyer Programme
FIT	Foreign Independent Traveller
GDS	Global Distribution System
GST	Goods and Services Tax
HBA	Hotel Booking Agent
HBAA	Hotel Bookings Agents Association
HBO	Hand Baggage Only
HROT	Hotel Room Occupancy Tax
IATA	International Air Transport Association
LH	Long Haul
LNR	Locally Negotiated Rate
LRA	Last Room Availability
MI	Management Information
OCC	Occupancy
OTM	Online Travel Management
PNR	Passenger Name Records

RFP	Request for Proposal
RO	Room Only
ROI	Return on Investment
RR	Room Rate
RR	Rack Rate
SBT	Self-Booking Tools
SH	Short Haul
SLA	Service Level Agreement
SRP	Special Rate Plan
TEM	Travel & Expense Management
TMC	Travel Management Company
VAT	Value Added Tax
WTM	World Travel Market

Wi-Fi for the business traveller

Today's business traveller is heavily dependent upon accessing their email account, calendar, company network and the internet, when they are in transit or overnighting at a hotel. To do so, travellers need fast and reliable access to Wi-Fi.   Wi-Fi (meaning wireless internet connectivity) is an important consideration for the business traveller, without it your executive will find it impossible to work effectively. A mobile device connection (such as your executive's mobile phone) may be adequate, but problems can arise when the mobile signal becomes weak, or when travelling in a different country. To overcome these issues, business travellers become dependent upon a local Wi-Fi connection, perhaps at the hotel they are staying in, the airport terminal they are travelling through, or at a café whilst grabbing a quick coffee. A local Wi-Fi connection can improve speed, connectivity, and resolve data download problems.

Having a good Wi-Fi connection also allows the business traveller to connect with their family (whilst away from home), by using Skype, Face Time, Google

Hangouts or Viber. The road warrior can say 'Hi' to the children from the comfort of their own hotel room, providing the signal is strong. Another common use of Wi-Fi for hotel guests, is to access movies across a variety of providers, as opposed to the hotel's in-house service, which can be expensive. Many hotels offer complimentary Wi-Fi in public areas, but some charge for in-room connectivity. Personally, I would avoid booking a hotel which charges its guests for in-room Wi-Fi. It's an outdated practice and should be inclusive of the room rate.

Airports have thankfully stopped charging travellers for Wi-Fi usage, and allow a set amount of minutes for free, whilst at the airport. Registration is usually required via the internet, but that can be completed before travelling to save time.

London airports Wi-Fi services

Airport	Wi-Fi allowance
London City	Free - unlimited
London Heathrow	4 hours free
London Gatwick	90 minutes free
London Luton	30 minutes free
London Stanstead	60 minutes free

Check with your executive's preferred hotels what their policy is on in-room Wi-Fi. Also research the connection available at airports where your executive is passing through, see if pre-registration is required for complementary Wi-Fi. Complete the registration on your executive's behalf prior to their travel.

A recent development is inflight Wi-Fi connectivity, allowing passengers to connect to onboard Wi-Fi whilst travelling by air. Unfortunately, traveller feedback is mixed. Connection can be slow, problematic or just doesn't work. Most airlines charge an additional fee to use this service, and it isn't cheap. Until the existing issues are resolved, it's best not to rely on inflight Wi-Fi, and instead use the check-in time to download everything which is required before boarding.

Another means of connecting whilst in transit are **Wi-Fi hotspots**. Wi-Fi hotspots allow your executive to access the internet whilst out and about, often for free. You'll find Wi-Fi hotspots dotted around most towns and cities, at various private and public locations. These tend to be open hotspots that anyone can join, and are usually free. Wi-Fi hotspots can be found in most populated areas – in cafes and restaurants, at train and underground stations, in libraries and even on buses. Registration is usually required in order to get a connection, and the period of 'free' time may be limited. Benefits for the business traveller include:

- Getting online easily when out and about
- Ability to stream and watch TV/video content at thousands of hotspots (news, presentations, company videos etc.)
- Avoid eating into a mobile data allowance
- Avoid data download fees

There are several apps and websites available, to search for free Wi-Fi hotspots. Whilst it's great to find a free wireless network accessible to everybody, open hotspots aren't as secure as private ones, so be wary of entering sensitive information when connected to one, and urge your executive to avoid using bank or credit cards on open Wi-Fi networks.

Ask your manager if he/she has adequate Wi-Fi connectivity when travelling. What problems have they experienced? Raise any technical issues with your local IT support team.

If your executive can't get free Wi-Fi, they can try **tethering** via their mobile phone. Tethering is when you turn you smartphone into a portable Wi-Fi hotspot, and use that to connect your laptop or tablet to the internet. Once you've turned tethering on, any device with a wireless connection can connect to the internet via your smartphone's connection.

Check your company's policy on tethering. It may be disabled on your mobile tariff. If it is enabled, any data your exec uses whilst tethering will come out of their monthly allowance, so make sure they watch how much they're using.

Tethering is quite successful when travelling via rail. I often travel via train and have tried unsuccessfully many times to get a stable connection with onboard Wi-Fi. The last time I used tethering it only dropped once, on a 3 hour journey.

Dropbox is the equivalent of an online memory stick. It's a free tool that gives you access to your folders online. Any file you save to your Dropbox will automatically save to all your computers, phones, and even the Dropbox platform (when configured), meaning you can access your files when away from the office, which is great for business travellers.

Business travel news

The business travel industry is a forever changing environment. Airlines alter their routes seasonally, new hotel groups are launched, hotel chains merge and re-brand, and airline alliances evolve. As bookers of business travel, it's important to keep abreast of industry news. Sign up for business travel communications, which are relevant to your executive's travel dashboard.

Google 'business travel magazine' and you will see the variety of publications available in this sector. Sign up for a publication which is free of charge, and relevant to your location. You could also follow your travel suppliers on Twitter, to receive updates in real time.

A publication I receive and highly recommend is 'the Business Travel Magazine' (published by BMI Publishing Ltd), which focuses on UK travel news. This gem of a publication is packed full of industry articles, and features, for bookers of business travel to absorb, all wrapped up in a lovely glossy exterior. A must have subscription for bookers of UK business travel. The publishers also host an annual conference in London 'the Business Travel Conference'. This event combines a full conference programme, with a business travel exhibition. Delegate numbers are limited to 200 so apply early for a place.

 If you are regularly booking business travel for your **road warrior** - attending a conference, exhibition or seminar on business travel should be part of your annual routine.

For travel news specific to your manager's business travel, subscribe to your hub airport's communication channels. Routes operated by your hub airport will change, dependent upon the winter or summer season. Timetables also change seasonally, to allow for the increased demand in flights during the holiday seasons. For the latest travel advice by country including safety and security, entry requirements, travel warnings and health, check out **www.gov.uk/foreign-travel-advice** (the UK Government website).

Alternatives to business travel

Your executive may be exhausted come the end of the working week. He or she may have travelled 1,000s of miles, spent 3 nights in different hotels, and didn't arrive home to see their family until 8pm on a Friday night. Itineraries such as these aren't sustainable long term, they can be damaging to your executive who isn't obtaining a work/life balance, and the cost implications to your company can be enormous over a 12 month period. Alternatives to business travel include working from home (therefore avoiding the commute into the office), and using virtual meeting solutions to replace face-to-face meetings, such as video, teleconferencing or web hosted (online) meetings.

Suggest a virtual meeting, when you consider one to be a viable option. Help your manager to reduce his/her travel, if at all possible, and enjoy more of a work/life balance.

If your executive is a road warrior, try and schedule a 'work from home' day in the diary, once a week. Arrange all of the meetings on that day to be either calls, or online meetings, so your boss doesn't have to travel, but can work from home effectively.

Smartphones get smarter every year, but battery life doesn't seem to get any better. If your exec needs to keep their mobile, tablet or other USB-powered device - going all day, they'll need a power bank. Power banks are pocket sized devices, which serve as an extra battery or external charger. Ensure you purchase a power bank which is compatible with the correct devices.

9

The City of London for the Business Executive

What's in this chapter?

The City of London is definitely where it's at! London is the largest city in Europe, and one of the most thriving business capitals in the world. Its home to the most successful companies in the UK, and business is booming. The City of London is a highly developed, concentrated area, and home to many leading finance, broking, insurance, legal, accounting and banking professionals. If you aren't supporting an executive based in London, then it's highly probable that your exec will travel to London, to meet with professionals who are. The fact that London has 5 airports is a testament to the enormous amount of commerce, which takes place in this world class city. Whether your exec uses air travel to reach London, or is a daily commuter, expanding your knowledge of the City is beneficial. In order to support your exec at the highest level, you should be familiar with London's facilities, the underground rail service, the financial districts, the best restaurants, hotels and serviced apartments. In this chapter we will explore:

- The City of London
- The London underground
- Postcodes in the City
- Business breakfast, lunch or dinner?
- Recommended restaurants
- Hotels in the City of London
- Recommended hotels
- Serviced apartments in the City of London
- Recommended serviced apartments
- Tipping in London
- Wi-Fi in the City of London

The City of London

The **City** is an area within London and it is important to distinguish between 'City' and 'London'. **London** refers to a much wider area across the capital, whereas **City** is the term used to describe the concentrated business district (which is just over 1 square mile in area), and is colloquially referred to as the **Square Mile.** Over half of the UK's highest ranking listed companies (the FTSE 100), and over 100 of Europe's top 500 companies, have headquarters in central London. American Express, Marriot Hotels, Ernst and Young, AXA, Deloitte, LinkedIn, and Uber all have a presence in the City. With a resident population of only 10,000, approximately 400,000 people work there on a daily basis.

London is one of the pre-eminent financial centres of the world, and vies with New York City as the most important location for international finance. The London Stock Exchange (the 3rd largest exchange globally), is based in Paternoster Square, close to St Paul's Cathedral.

London is a recognised meeting point - both for UK based execs and for execs visiting from overseas. And as London is home to the majority of the UK's registered head offices, it's naturally the base for a vast number of CEOs, CFOs, Company Founders, Presidents and Board Members. Considering London's global importance, it's essential to build your knowledge up, as you never know when your exec will be required to attend a client or investor meeting, conference, trade show, contract negotiation or networking event in this fabulous city.

The **Square Mile** (the informal name for the City of London) is roughly the area bordered by Liverpool Street, Tower Hill, Blackfriars and Barbican tube stations (see image over). The Square Mile (or City) is on the northern side of the River Thames. Dragons mark the City's major entrances, such as at Temple Bar, and black bollards bearing the Square Mile's flag, coat of arms and Latin motto "Domine dirige nos" - "Lord, guide us" – signify the boundaries of the City. Within the Square Mile are several iconic buildings which have become synonymous with London. Steeped in history, you will find St Pauls Cathedral, London Bridge, the Tower of London, Monument, the Old Bailey, Leadenhall

Market and the Bank of England. Which jostle for attention amongst the stunning modern designs of the Lloyds Building, Heron Tower, Tower 42, 30 St Mary Axe (the Gherkin), 20 Fenchurch Street (the Walkie Talkie) and 122 Leadenhall Street (the Cheese Grater). Londoners do love allocating nicknames to their skyscrapers! The Square Mile is a truly interesting place to visit, and if time permits, your business exec should view the amazing architecture, old and new, whilst in London.

Map of the Square Mile

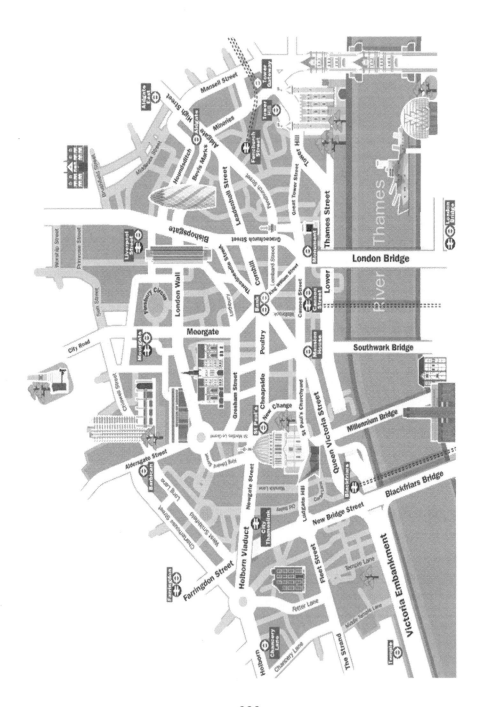

The London underground

Getting around the City of London is similar to that in any capital city – it has an underground rail system – or subway. London Underground's history dates back to 1863 when the world's first underground railway, the Metropolitan Railway, opened between Paddington and Farringdon serving 6 intermediate stations. Since then the underground network, (affectionately nicknamed 'the Tube' by generations of Londoners), has grown to 270 stations and 11 lines stretching deep into the Capital's suburbs, and beyond. The Square Mile is predominately served by the Central, Circle, District, Hammersmith and City lines. See image below of the tube stations in the Square Mile.

Using the underground can often be quicker than using a taxi, however, allow for an often overcrowded system which takes time to access and exit in peak periods. On a positive note, trains are frequent, are cost effective for travellers, and the stations have Wi-Fi. Virgin Media operates London Underground Wi-Fi and it is available at 250 stations. You can go online anywhere in those stations

- in ticket halls, corridors and platforms. There's no signal in tunnels, but your phone will connect to the signal at the next Wi-Fi enabled platform so you can pick up where you left off. Customers of Virgin Media, EE, Vodafone, O2 and Three can access the service for FREE. If your exec isn't with one of those providers, you can purchase a daily, weekly or monthly, Virgin Media Wi-Fi Pass to get online. Connecting is easy – make sure your device's Wi-Fi is switched on and you should connect automatically when entering the station. If not, select your providers Wi-Fi from the Wi-Fi options shown on your phone.

Purchasing paper tickets for rail travel can be expensive, and so can a day travelcard at £12.50. It's more cost effective to purchase an **Oyster card** for your exec and access the daily capping rate of £6.50 for unlimited Zone 1 and 2 travel. This can be completed online via the Transport for London website. An Oyster card is a plastic smartcard which can hold credit for your journeys. You can use an Oyster card to travel on the bus, Tube, tram, DLR, London Overground, TfL Rail, Emirates Air Line, River Bus services and most National Rail services in London. It's a no brainer – when in London, journeys in central London (zone 1), are more than 50% cheaper with an Oyster card. PAs can be super-efficient by arranging for an Oyster card – prior to your exec's visit to London. Create an Oyster card online account and access the following services:

- Check what's on your Oyster card
- Top up your pay as you go credit and add or renew Travelcards
- Set up Auto top-up
- Protect your Oyster card
- See your Oyster journey history (great for expense claims)
- Apply for a refund for incomplete journeys

Once your exec is in receipt of their Oyster card, they will enjoy easy and quick access through the barriers (no need to queue for travel tickets). Purchase a standard Oyster card to access the online management and journey history. If your exec is not a repeat traveller to London then purchase a Visitor Oyster card which contains discounts for leisure and tourist attractions on top.

Visit www.tfl.gov.uk (Transport for London) for all your London transport enquiries. Download a tube map, purchase an Oyster card, plan a journey – using the journey tool, which will map out the best mode of transport for your executive's route across town.

Postcodes in the City

Each district, within the City, has its own postcode. The London EC (Eastern Central) carries 4 different EC codes and each code corresponds with the different districts within the City. For example:

Postcode prefix	Area
EC1	Clerkenwell, Barbican
EC2	Moorgate, Liverpool Street, Cheapside, Bank
EC3	Aldgate, Monument, Tower Hill, Leadenhall Street, London Bridge
EC4	Fleet Street, St Pauls, Temple, Blackfriars

Postcode areas are also visible on street signs in the City.

 Searching for hotels and restaurants in London can be daunting if you don't know the area. Use London postcodes to narrow your online search results, by using the postcode of your execs meeting point as the search reference. So say your exec's meeting address is 122 Leadenhall St, London EC3V 4AB – enter EC3V 4AB into the search fields. All the hotels or restaurants returned will be closeby to your execs meeting location.

Business breakfast, lunch or dinner?

When in London a breakfast, lunch or dinner appointment is highly likely. Travelling to London on business can be expensive, so it's important your exec maximises their time whilst there, and meets with their key business contacts. If your executive asks you to make the arrangements, it's very important to carefully source the correct venue, location and price bracket - to match the attendees, subject matter and objective of the meeting. Consider your execs requirements: is this an informal bite to eat with a colleague, or a formal fine dining lunch with a client or prospect? Is the appointment with your execs line manager, or a C-suite associate? Is lunch required on a 1 to 1 basis or with a wider group? Is this an introduction type meeting or is the relationship already well established?

Introduction meetings are rarely scheduled over lunch – they are allocated a smaller time slot, requiring less financial outlay and generally take up a breakfast or mid morning coffee slot. In London, it's appropriate to schedule 'breakfast' meetings, which are less formal but encourage new business relationships. Due to travel time into London, breakfast meetings should be scheduled between 0830-1000. It's advisable to check if your chosen venue accepts bookings for breakfast reservations, many City venues do.

Lunch in a high end City restaurant is reserved for the more serious stuff – schmoozing the client, adding the finer points to a multi-million pound contract deal, or discussing an additional professional service your company wishes to bolt onto an existing contract. Dinner in the City is more exclusive and generally for existing contacts, because you are imposing on an individual's personal time. Dinners in London are expensive events to host, and are often held in private dining rooms to ensure sensitive matters cannot be overhead, and to guarantee everyone's focus and attention. Big money is thrown at corporate private dining events, but the business being hunted can be a fantastic return on investment – if it comes off!

Recommended restaurants

The Square Mile has, in recent years, become recognised for its vast choice of restaurants for the discerning business executive. The British Olympics 2012 generated new interest and investment, due to the increased number of global visitors. The concentrated number of restaurants to choose from, can make sourcing the correct venue for a business breakfast, client lunch or dinner a challenging task. New venues open on a regular basis, with much hype and publicity, but the stalwarts have secured a loyal customer base and have reputations to match. In London, areas are over developed, tall buildings tower above the pavements, and you have to crane your neck in order to see sky. When placing a meeting at a restaurant think about natural light, views and space between tables – to create a positive ambience for your dining guests. I, personally, recommend the following restaurants in the City of London - these restaurants are well situated, provide a reputable service, can be booked with confidence, and are ideal for your business executive's breakfast, lunch or dinner.

Angler, 3 South Place, London, EC2M 2AF

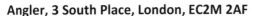

2 mins walk to Moorgate tube, 6 mins to Liverpool Street tube. Seafood cuisine served at the top of the South Place Hotel. Angler combines an elegant dining room with a sophisticated menu for City diners. The Michelin-starred restaurant showcases sustainable seafood from British waters, paired with the best seasonal and local produce. Situated on the 7th floor, the restaurant has floor to ceiling windows commanding fabulous City views. The café is subtly upmarket, with comfy striped chairs and a foliage-effect mirror running the length of the dining room. A rooftop terrace provides alfresco dining with a more casual menu. Great for summer drinks or cocktails with clients.

Coq d'Argent, No.1 Poultry, London, EC2R 8EJ

1 minute from Bank tube. Classic French cuisine served in a choice of either the brasserie or restaurant (for more formal dining). A stunning roof garden provides panoramic views across the City and is an oasis in the summer. Great for travelling executives who are new to London, who can combine lunch with a drink in the roof top gardens, whilst enjoying the views of the City of London. Also a fantastic spot for corporate entertainment, and early evening drinks in summer. Gets extremely busy – always book in advance.

 Wherever your exec visits regularly, it's a good idea to build up your knowledge of suitable restaurants in that city for business lunches. See if there is a restaurant directory for that location or an online search tool. Check out restaurant reviews on Trip Advisor (or similar) prior to booking.

The Royal Exchange, London, EC3V 3LR
The Royal Exchange is located in a prime position opposite the Bank of England and Bank tube station. Originally the City's largest trading floor, the Royal Exchange is a landmark venue and has 3 different dining options. An institution for all business professionals within the Square Mile, and one which you should utilise to impress. The 3 distinctive dining areas are:

The Grand Café: on entering the main building you will find the Grand Café occupying the centre of the courtyard on the ground floor. The centre piece is a chic oval bar with gleaming brass countertop, which serves a selection of seafood, and offers an all-day dining menu. Waiting staff buzz around in smart aprons, providing impeccable service. This location is pure theatre, classic architecture with a real buzz of city life. I have arranged many a breakfast meeting at this venue, it's very popular and provides the perfect backdrop for providing inspiration and energy. The Grand Café is available on first come first served basis (you cannot reserve tables).

The Threadneedle Bar and Gallery: overlooks the Grand Café, so provides the atmosphere and buzz of the location but in slightly quieter surroundings. Open at lunchtimes, the Gallery serves the Grand Café food menu. The Threadneedle provides an excellent option between the hustle and bustle atmosphere of the Grand Café, and the formal dining of Sauterelle.

Sauterelle: is situated on the mezzanine level of the Royal Exchange. This fine dining establishment offers contemporary cuisine, in an intimate and more formal atmosphere. The restaurant design is elegant and chic, the glazed arches offer spectacular views of both the Bank of England, and the historic courtyard below. With a price tag to match, Sauterelle is perfect for executive level lunch meetings on a 1 to 1 basis, or closing that deal with celebratory fine dining, in superb surroundings in a truly memorable location.

 The Grand Café is one of my favourite venues for business meetings. For execs visiting from overseas it really should feature on their list of places to 'lunch' at whilst in London. It's superb.

229

Smiths of Smithfield, 67-77 Charterhouse Street, London, EC1M 6HJ

2 mins walk from Farringdon tube station, 5 mins walk to Barbican tube station. Smiths of Smithfield is a 4 floor eatery boasting 2 restaurants, a cafe and bar. There's a definite New York feel to the overall style, with plenty of open spaces, blasted brickwork, big windows and comfy leather seating. The roof top restaurant (and terrace) is great for formal business dining, and the terrace commands panoramic city views. Smiths of Smithfield is located opposite the famous Smithfield Market – London's only working meat market in a very historic part of London. With cuisine to suit its location, the menu includes rare breed beef, butchered and cut in house. For business lunches or dinners, ensure that your reservation is with the top floor restaurant.

TOP TIPS

Opentable.co.uk is a free to use online booking service, for top restaurants in many worldwide cities. You can search for London restaurants by area e.g. Bank, Farringdon, London Bridge and Liverpool Street. Collect reward points for bookings made and honoured, and redeem them for personal dining rewards or gifts.

Hawksmoor Guildhall 10 Basinghall Street, London, EC2V 5BQ

4 mins walk to Bank tube, 6 mins to Moorgate tube. The Hawksmoor operate several restaurants in London - but the Hawksmoor Guildhall is slap bang in the Square Mile. A haven for carnivores, and much favoured by city gents with big appetites, and a penchant for steaks. The Guildhall offers a comprehensive breakfast menu – great for the early morning meeting in the City. For breakfast, think an enormous Full English (for 2 to share), which includes Smoked bacon chop, sausages, (made with pork, beef, & mutton), black pudding, short-rib bubble & squeak, grilled bone marrow, trotter baked beans, fried eggs, grilled mushrooms, roast tomatoes, HP gravy, and unlimited toast. If your exec can move after eating all that – that's an impressive feat in itself! There are smaller breakfast options for those with smaller appetites, and a concern for their cholesterol levels.

Add to bible...

Add details of your preferred restaurants (by city) to your bible. Include the postal or zip address for quick identification of district, and comments for when to use e.g. formal, informal, lunch or dinner.

1 Lombard Street Brasserie, London EC3V 9AA

Opposite Bank tube station, 4 mins walk from Monument tube station. A former bank building, housing a modern European brasserie, and circular bar with domed skylight. 1 Lombard Street is the Square Mile's most established restaurant, and arguably its best placed. Situated in pole position next to Mansion House, the official residence of the Lord Mayor of the City of London, and directly opposite the Bank of England. Casually elegant, warm and inviting, it features the building's stunning glass copula (a centre piece dome), which houses The Dome Bar. Open for breakfast, lunch and dinner, 5 days a week, the bustling 200 seater brasserie is suited to all tastes, budgets and occasions.

Hotels in the City of London

There are hundreds of hotels to choose from, within central London. However, all hotels are generally at premium prices due to their location in this financial district. The City of London attracts a blend of both tourists, and business travellers, on a daily basis. Business travellers provide the majority of custom throughout the working week, whilst the tourist trade dominates at weekends. For many years there were no hotels at all in the City - even though the financial firms in the City were one of the most lucrative sources of custom. In recent years, the shortfall has been addressed, and over 1,000 hotel rooms have been created within the Square Mile. Hotel rates from Monday to Thursday will be at a premium in the City. Rates tend to decrease on Friday and Saturday as the City ceases trading, and business people leave to travel back to their families at their residential locations.

London hotel rates fluctuate daily, and it is possible to secure discounted rates across the city, which are released as **late availability** offers online. Best available rates or last minute rates can save you £££s (if you can grab them).

Check comparison and last minute websites for best available hotel rates. Your travel management company may not list all rates in London if you are based in another country, so shop around to ensure you have been offered a competitive rate for your exec in London. **www.LateRooms.co.uk** is a useful site when searching for London hotel rooms.

If your executive has travelled into the city on business from overseas, or has travelled extensively across the UK to get to London, consider securing accommodation within the City area. Cheaper accommodation can be found across Greater London, but the commute to the meeting the next morning could offset any savings made, in terms of distance from their meeting point, travel costs and time and inefficiency for the traveller. If you are not sure of the London area your executive is travelling to – obtain the full postal address of the meeting place and Google it. Note the postcode (as we discussed previously), and use the postcode when searching for a nearby hotel.

Utilise Google maps for the meeting point and your hotel options. Note the distance, use the direction tool available and note the time taken to travel between the two on foot, road and rail. For example, your executive has a meeting at 30 St Mary Axe (the Gherkin) and you've located the Montcalm at the Brewery London City, as a potentially suitable hotel. Enter the meeting location into Google maps, then use the directions tool to enter the hotel address. The search results will reveal that the Montcalm Hotel is 9 mins by taxi, 14 mins by tube and 18 mins on foot to the Gherkin. 9 mins by taxi is perfectly acceptable for your business exec, and probably the best option if they have luggage. You can always cross check recommended journey times by using the transport for London website.

Ideally I would secure a hotel for my executive within 15 mins travel time to their meeting. Using that radius in London, will free up hotels in other locations which are in cheaper postal districts - but offer perfectly adequate accommodation for the business traveller.

Always ensure that your exec's accommodation requirements are met, and that the location is convenient for the following day's meetings. Minimise any potential travel disasters by doing your research on the location of the meeting, and the distance to the hotel. If the commute is minimal and the accommodation is within budget, and appropriate for your traveller, you have found a suitable place for your business executive to stay.

If your executive expects high standards of accommodation when staying in the City of London, consider the hotels overleaf.

Recommended hotels

Apex London Wall 4★, 9 Copthall Avenue, London, EC2R 7NJ

Nearest tubes: Moorgate 4 mins walk, Bank 5 mins walk. Apex London Wall is a luxury 4 star hotel, located in the heart of the business and financial district close to the Bank of England, St Paul's Cathedral and Royal Exchange. Also nearby are The Gherkin and Barbican Arts Centre. One of the newest hotels near London Wall , the hotel features include a bar, restaurant (Off the Wall), outside bar and dining area, fitness centre and 89 stylish bedrooms, some with a private balcony Complementary in-room Wi-Fi, luxury toiletries, widescreen LCD TVs and 24-hour room service. The hotel's common spaces all feature contemporary design touches, and bold-yet-tasteful textures.

Subscribe online for your preferred hotel supplier's news, by subscribing to their email newsletter. Keep up to date with new openings, hotel offers and new services. You never know – they may invite you to their next hotel or bar launch!

DoubleTree by Hilton Hotel London, Tower of London 4★
7 Pepys Street, London, EC3N 4AF

Tower Hill tube 3 mins walk. Contemporary London hotel in the centre of the financial district. 583 bedrooms, each guest room boasts floor to ceiling windows (which open) ensuring a room with a view for all. Complimentary Wi-Fi throughout the hotel, with an iMac in every standard guest and deluxe room. Fitness centre, rooftop Sky lounge with views over the London skyline. Executive rooms and suites offer complimentary breakfast, afternoon drinks and snacks in the Executive Lounge, plus 55-inch TVs. Located close to the Tower of London, Tower Bridge, St Katharine's Docks, and Fenchurch Street Station. Loyalty card program: Hilton Hhonors.

Add to bible... Add details of your executive's preferred hotels, by City, to your bible. Include the postal address or zip code for quick identification of the area. Include comments which could be useful when booking next time e.g. close to a particular client's office, quiet location, good levels of service etc. Also record any hotels to avoid in your bible and why.

Grange St Pauls 5★, 10 Godliman Street, London, EC4V 5AJ

St Pauls tube 5 mins walk, Mansion House 6 mins walk, Blackfriars 6 mins. A 5 star hotel, perfectly located in the heart of the City's financial district, close to St Pauls Cathedral. A spectacular Atrium, 80 feet through the centre of the hotel, giving rise to a choice of restaurants and bars. 433 guest bedrooms, all offering high-speed complimentary Wi-Fi and broadband, air conditioning, 24-hour room service, mini-bar, trouser press, in-room safe, and tea/coffee-making facilities as standard. Leisure facilities including health club, 18m swimming pool, Jacuzzi and steam room. The hotel also has 2 expansive floors of meeting and events space, and a dedicated Business Centre with PC workstations, print and fax facilities for business travellers.

South Place Hotel 5★, 3 South Place, London EC2M 2AF

Moorgate 3 mins walk. South Place, a new Hotel in the City of London, is the first purpose-built hotel to open in the Square Mile in 100 years. Providing 80 bedrooms, complimentary Wi-Fi, 4 bars, 5 private dining rooms and 2 restaurants (all are iconic Conran design). The South Place Hotel is home to the Angler restaurant which serves some of the finest seafood in London and boasts a Michelin star. The Angler rooftop terrace is one of the most popular spots for alfresco eating and drinking in London. The contemporary interior provides an alternative to more 'traditional' type hotel accommodation in the City. A great alternative for the business traveller. Named as one of the Big Six Art hotels worldwide.

Threadneedles Hotel 5★, 5 Threadneedles Street, London, EC2R 8AY

Bank 3 mins walk, Monument 7 mins walk. This former Victorian bank is now a boutique hotel and is located in the heart of the financial district. Discreetly tucked behind Bank tube station, this 5 star retreat provides a luxurious, peaceful and chic escape. Housed in a beautifully converted banking hall built in 1856, the awe-inspiring stained glass circular atrium is spectacular, and the bedrooms are seductive and well equipped. Within easy reach are popular landmarks such as St Paul's Cathedral, The Barbican, Shakespeare's Globe and the Tower of London. 74 rooms, complimentary in-room Wi-Fi.

 Most executives have a preference on hotel style, be it contemporary, traditional, cutting edge design or quirky. Find out your exec's hotel style and try and match the hotel accordingly.

 What does your exec expect from their hotel facilities? Do they need a fast Wi-Fi connection, laundry service, in room dining service? Get to know your execs expectations and meet them when selecting your hotel.

The Montcalm at the Brewery London City 5★
52 Chiswell Street, London EC1Y 4SA

Barbican tube 6 mins walk, Moorgate tube 6 mins walk. The Montcalm at the Brewery (don't let the name put you off) wears its quirky heritage with pride. An award-winning transformation from historic brewery to handsome 5 star hotel. With period features at every turn, it stays faithful to its past, as the 18th century base of Whitbread & Co, but it's also every inch the 21st century hotel you'd expect of a superbly central City of London location. A refreshing blend of elegance and informality, it's the ideal urban retreat, welcoming wide-eyed explorers and time-pressed business travellers alike, to the true heart of London. A truly gorgeous hotel.

Serviced apartments in the City of London

An alternative option to hotel accommodation in the City (and most European cities) are serviced apartments. Serviced apartments are great for longer stays, they provide greater privacy, a larger space (often with a lounge area or sofa) and come equipped with a small kitchen/dining area with a table you can work from. Room service is not to be expected - if in-room dining is required by your executive choose a hotel, and consider the serviced apartment as the self-catering option. However, perhaps your exec prefers to cook their own meals, or has special dietary requirements, and so preparing their own dinner won't be a problem. Some providers will leave a welcome box of goodies in the apartment, on arrival. These will contain the essentials of tea, coffee, milk, fruit juice and cereal, as well as a few treats. Catering boxes can also be pre-ordered via the provider's website, so that they are in the room, awaiting your exec's arrival. The apartment provider will also advise you where the nearest convenience store is, so your exec can buy additional ingredients for dinner, should they choose to eat in.

If your exec wants to stay in one evening, and doesn't wish to cook, try Deliveroo.co.uk for restaurant food delivered to your door. Get amazing food from an incredible selection of local restaurants, delivered in an average of just 32 minutes. Use the app for quick ordering when in transit. Deliveroo does not use low quality takeaway style restaurants, so food should be well received by your exec after a hard day in the City.

Recommended serviced apartments

Market View, West Smithfield, London, EC1A 9HY (by BridgeStreet)
Located in the heart of the City of London, close to Hatton Garden, Market View is a fully refurbished, Victorian, red brick property dating back to 1907 and proudly retains many external period features to date. Within easy walking distance to St Paul's Cathedral by the River Thames it provides stunning views of the City of London skyline. The building comprises of 65 studios, 1, 2 and 3 bedroom corporate apartments. Located in the heart of London's historic Smithfield Market, the apartments are a short walk to St Pauls, Smithfield Market, Aldersgate Street, Barbican and Farringdon tubes. Additionally, Market View is close to the Haberdashers Hall, an established corporate events venue.

The Kings Wardrobe, Wardrobe Place, London, EC4V 5AF (by BridgeStreet)
Kings Wardrobe apartments are located in a tranquil courtyard behind St Pauls
Cathedral, in the heart of the City. A selection of 69 studio, 1, 2 and 3 bed fully
furnished apartments, are very convenient for meetings in the Square Mile. The
elegant 5 star Residences are furnished to a high standard and styled in line with
the Grade I listed building. In-apartment technology means high specification
audio and visual, Wi-Fi and i-Pod docking stations.

Atelier, Greville Street, London, EC1N 8AF (by BridgeStreet) is a 5 star,
environmentally friendly apartment development close to Hatton Gardens,
London's thriving 'Jewellery Quarter' (or was before the heist of 2015!). A 2-
minute walk from the Farringdon train station and a 6 minute walk from the
Chancery Lane Underground station, these contemporary boutique apartments
are a 4 minute walk from a grocery store and multiple restaurants. Luxe studios,
1 and 2 bedroom apartments featuring full kitchens with dishwashers and
microwaves include flat-screen TVs, DVD players, washer/dryers and Wi-Fi, plus
high-end furnishings and decor.

Citadines Barbican 7-21 Goswell Rd, City of London, EC1M 7AH (by the Ascott Limited). Citadines Barbican is excellently located for the City, and is walking distance to Aldersgate Street, Barbican tube station, Charterhouse Square and St Pauls. From a studio for 1 or 2 people to 1 bedroom apartments which can sleep up to 4, it is up to you to choose the type of accommodation that suits. Whichever you choose, all serviced apartments have a fully-equipped kitchen, a TV with cable channels and free high speed Wi-Fi. Weekly housekeeping is free, but you can also opt for housekeeping on demand. Laundry services and breakfast are also available as options.

Marlin Queen Street, 30 Queen Street, London, EC4R 1BR
Marlin Queen Street is situated in a great location in the heart of London's financial district, moments from the London Stock Exchange, the Bank of England and Paternoster Square. Cannon Street and Mansion House tube stations are closest. Queen Street lies just a few minutes' walk away from One New Change shopping centre, featuring quality restaurants which includes Gordon Ramsay's Bread Street Kitchen. Studio and 1, 2 bedroomed apartments available.

Always use London postcodes to narrow search results, when sourcing serviced apartments in London. Several websites can mislead on location. An 'EC' postcode prefix indicates the apartment is within the City of London.

Add to bible...

Add your preferred 'Serviced Apartments' to your bible, for future reference. Note your executive's feedback from previous stays including proximity to meetings, ease of use, logistics and parking. Note local convenience stores and catering delivery services.

Tipping in London

Restaurants

A service charge is an amount added to your bill before it is given to you, and is almost always based on a percentage of the bill. This is not a tax, it relates to the service you have received by the waiting staff. If it is "discretionary" or "suggested" you are free to either pay the amount or to decline payment. For larger group dining, a service charge payment may be mandatory. If your restaurant is billing you a service charge – there is no requirement to leave a cash tip on the table. If a service charge is not evident on your bill, then leave a cash tip on the table for around 10% of the total bill (if the service received has been good). Although restaurants should make their in-house policy clear, it's worth checking with the waiter that he/she will personally receive the tip or service charge, rather than the company, particularly if paying by credit card. If you have been unhappy with the service, you shouldn't leave a tip, and decline to pay the service charge fee. Tipping isn't necessary for fast food, self-service or takeaway meals.

Hotels

The process is the same if you are dining in a hotel restaurant. If there isn't a service charge added to your bill in a hotel restaurant, it's customary to leave a cash tip on the table (10% of the bill). For room cleaning staff (housekeeping), the guest can leave an amount of their choosing in the bedroom. Tips for other

hotel staff such as concierges and door staff are discretionary, and are most commonplace for porters. Similar to anywhere in the world, a porter bringing your bags to your room expects to receive a cash tip. Around £2 would be reasonable. You should not tip room service for bringing food/drinks to your room. London hotels charge a 'tray charge' for room service, so you will be charged for this privilege on your invoice at checkout. This varies from £5-£10. Tray charges can be found in the small print of the hotel in-room dining menu.

Bars and Pubs

People generally do not tip in pubs in London, but may offer to buy a drink for the bartender who will either have it then, save it for later, or keep the price of the drink as a tip. Bartenders sometimes hand back change on a tipping tray, although it's still up to the customer to choose to leave a tip.

Wi-Fi in the City of London

The City of London became the first global financial capital to offer free, unlimited, Wi-Fi in outdoor areas in December 2012. Wi-Fi is provided by 'The Cloud'. The Cloud's City Wi-Fi network covers 95% of the Square Mile's outdoor areas, and **unlimited free access** is now available to all users. The area covered is around 1.1 square miles, bordered by the River Thames to the south, Barbican to the north, Aldgate in the east and Chancery Lane to the west. Users should expect maximum speeds of around 5Mbps.

The City of London for the business executive

If your executive is visiting London for meetings, and requires Wi-Fi connectivity whilst in transit, complete the online pre-registration to The Cloud before they travel. This will enable quicker connectivity when in London. **www.thecloud.net.**

When in London connect using the instructions below.

① Check your WiFi is on

② Select The Cloud from the available network list

③ Open your web browser

④ Click the 'Get Online' button on The Cloud's landing page

⑤ Select The Cloud WiFi

WiFi Powered by
The Cloud
A BSkyB company

Free unlimited WiFi use across the Square Mile

Watch this short video for more information on Wi-Fi in the Square Mile. Open YouTube and enter '**Free unlimited Wi-Fi use across the Square Mile**' in the search box. The video is produced by the City of London Corporation.

Smartphone and tablet users can now access the network more easily by downloading The Cloud's "FastConnect" app, which will automatically connect users once they are in range of the network, and eliminates the need to re-enter credentials each time. The app is available for Apple, Android and Windows devices, and more details can be found at:

http://www.thecloud.net/free-wifi/get-the-app/

Recommended Websites

Alison.com

Find free online courses available with Alison.com. Alison is a global social enterprise, dedicated to providing free online training. Online you will find free Outlook training with video content, plus a host of other software courses. Also free courses on soft skills and personal development.

Airportguides.co.uk

A comprehensive resource for UK airport information. Including contact numbers for the Airport, a guide to shops and restaurants, facilities information, all in an easy to use format, viewable by location. Source regional airport information in one place.

Bookatable.com

Europe's largest online restaurant booking website, operating in 9 different languages and across 19 countries. Sign up for offers direct to your inbox and make free 'real-time' restaurant reservations, with instant confirmation, online. Bookatable enables you to browse restaurants based on location, cuisine and price point. In the UK for example, it provides restaurant recommendations for ALL major cities.

Bridgestreet.com

A leading international provider of serviced apartments, BridgeStreet and its Alliance members, offer over 50,000 corporate apartments in 60 countries across the globe. Corporate housing for individuals, corporations, families, and government travellers – all with the choice of BridgeStreet 'Residences', 'Serviced Apartments' or 'Suites'. Search and book online through Bridgestreet.com.

Citybaseapartments.com

Citybase Apartments is one of the UK's leading accommodation agents specialising in serviced apartments in London, throughout the UK and across the world. Our apartments are a great alternative to a hotel thanks to the space, value and freedom they offer. We have more than 10 years' experience providing apartments for all types of travellers, both business and leisure, and we work hard to make booking a serviced apartment simple.

Epaa.org.uk

Launched in 2016 The Executive & Personal Assistants Association is a new, dynamic, and innovative professional membership body for executive and personal assistants across the United Kingdom. View the website for a list of the UK regional PA networks, together with full contact details.

Deliveroo.co.uk

The home and office delivery option for restaurant food. Order online, via the app and enter your delivery postcode to see what's available in your area. Choose from a selection of good quality restaurants – not low quality takeaways. Use Deliveroo for catering delivered to your hotel room, serviced apartment or even the office, but don't forget the cutlery!

Dropbox.com

An extremely helpful tool for the business traveller. Dropbox is a free service that acts as a virtual memory stick. Dropbox allows the user to easily synchronise a file across different applications e.g. your laptop, tablet and phone. Any file you save to your Dropbox will automatically save to all your computers, phones and even the Dropbox platform. Don't risk losing your memory stick, save your files to your Dropbox for safe keeping on the cloud.

Executivepa.com

The website of the subscription based Executive PA magazine. Access the website for free. The role of the senior PA is critical in any business and Executive PA Magazine provides readers with essential information on all aspects of their career, from how to improve their job satisfaction, to advice on training and career development. Executive PA Magazine also brings readers interviews from high profile PAs and their bosses, and reports on new and exciting venues throughout the UK.

Recommended websites

Gov.uk/foreign-travel-advice
Travel advice from the UK Foreign Office. The site contains safety advice by Country, security advice for the business traveller, and what to do when things go wrong. Passport information, entry requirements per country, travel warnings, terrorism alerts and known health issues.

Flightstats.com
Global flight information for the business traveller. Overview of major global airports, real time flight information for departures and arrivals. Weather conditions, traveller ratings, flight tracker tool, ground transportation options and flight delay tracker.

Gcflearnfree.org
For more than a decade, the GCFLearnFree.org program has helped millions around the world learn the essential skills they need to live and work in the 21st century. From Microsoft Office and email to reading, math, and more. GCFLearnFree.org offers 125 tutorials, including more than 1,100 lessons, videos, and interactives, completely FREE.

Gonative.com
Search for serviced apartments by neighbourhood name, tube station or map. Online booking tool. Apartments include studios, 1 bed and 2 bed options. We operate more own brand, award-winning serviced apartments in London than any other operator – over 1,300 and growing. Our buildings range from boutique gems in cobbled streets and sympathetic refurbishments of historic buildings, to the very best of modern architecture.

ITM.org.uk
The Institute of Travel and Meetings is the leading professional body for buyers, managers and suppliers of business travel in the UK and Ireland. ITM Connect membership is free (entry level membership). ITM produces a variety of specialist travel and meetings reports on key industry topics, best practice travel and travel management.

Laterooms.com

LateRooms.com is a hotel reservations website providing late availability accommodation throughout the UK, Europe and the rest of the world. It allows both independent and chain hotel rooms to be booked online or by telephone, up to a year in advance or minutes before check-in. A valuable website when sourcing last minute accommodation, but particularly useful for securing late availability rates in central London hotels.

Linkedin.com

LinkedIn is the leading online business network for professionals and organisations. LinkedIn has over 400 million members in more than 200 countries, including executives from every Fortune 500 and FTSE 100 company. Individuals use LinkedIn for professional networking, connecting, and job searching. Companies use LinkedIn for recruiting, and advertising new job opportunities. Often used for headhunting purposes, members may be contacted directly by prospective employers or their representative.

Londoncityairport.com

London City Airport (LCY) is the only London airport situated in London itself. Just 3 miles from Canary Wharf, 7 miles from the City and 10 miles from London's West End, linked via the Docklands Light Railway. London City Airport's own Premier PA Club is an exclusive, FREE to join club open to London-based PAs, EAs and Office Managers. Offering airport showarounds, events, promotions and competitions for its PA members.

Nationalcareersservice.direct.gov.uk

The National Careers Service provides information, advice and guidance to help you make decisions on learning, training and work opportunities in England. The service offers confidential and impartial advice. This is supported by qualified careers advisers. Search the website for job descriptions, salary guides and projected salaries. Learning advice, course options, back to work guidance, and access to career service advisors is readily available.

Opentable.co.uk

An online restaurant reservation website, listing restaurant reviews. Restaurants are searchable by country and by city. OpenTable dining rewards is a frequent-diner programme that awards OpenTable points each time you honour a booking made via the website. When you earn enough points, you can redeem them for a dining cheque, usable at all OpenTable restaurants.

Pa-assist.com

Based in the UK with 12,000 registered users, online resources include supplier directories, venue finding, and office tools. PA-Assist emails regular newsletters to members, including diary dates for networking group events across the UK and Ireland, training events, promotional offers and industry news.

PAlife.co.uk

The free subscription magazine for UK PAs. PA Life caters for all market sectors. Our multi-channel distribution of news and analysis ensures all industry execs – from PA to the Manager, Director, CEO and Chairman – are served with the information they need to grow their business. PA Life has a unique position at the heart of the PA community. As such we build events that deliver targeted audiences for our partners' trade messages.

Squaremeal.co.uk

Square Meal is an independent guide to the best restaurants, venues and bars in London. Search by area, postcode, tube station or landmark. Filter by price, cuisine type or special offers. Complete restaurant reservations through the online booking tool and accrue points per booking. Redeem your points for rewards including beauty products and meal deals. Subscribe to regular newsletters to your inbox, or hard copy magazines (if you work in the central London area).

Support.office.com

Microsoft Office's own training centre with FREE downloadable training guides and FREE video training. Training is available for different versions of Outlook, amongst other Office applications, and different skill levels.

thebusinesstravelmagazine.co.uk

For buyers and arrangers of business travel and meetings. An excellent website full of business travel news, articles, features and tips. The Business Travel Magazine is published hard copy, bi-monthly. Subscriptions are FREE in the UK, and available for a fee outside of the UK.

theCloud.net

The free Wi-Fi provider in the City of London. Create a user account online to access free, unlimited Wi-Fi when in the City of London. Download the app 'FastConnect' for your smartphone or tablet. If your executive is visiting London for meetings and requires Wi-Fi connectivity whilst in transit, complete the online pre-registration prior to their travel. This will enable quicker connectivity on arrival.

Tiger-recruitment.co.uk

Tiger Recruitment has a reputation for placing many of the most senior executive assistant and personal assistant jobs in London. The client base is impressive and includes FTSE 100 Companies, Banks and UHNWIs. With offices in London and Dubai, Tiger match the top EA and PA candidates with the most sought after positions. Representing graduates, experienced EAs and those looking for international opportunities, talk to Tiger if you are considering your next career move.

Timeout.com

Restaurant reviews, search by area and book online (limited search options and functionality). Publishers of the London Eating and Drinking Guide (an annual publication available to purchase hardcopy) which is a useful reference manual if you are a regular restaurant booker in London.

Recommended websites

tfl.gov.uk

The website for Transport for London. For any public transport queries in London go to this site. It has the most up to date information regarding travel disruption, engineering works and an online payment system for the congestion charge. Download a tube map, purchase an Oyster card, plan a journey (using the journey tool) which will map out the best mode of transport for your executive's route across town.

Trip Advisor.co.uk

Reviews are uploaded by travellers and diners which therefore provide an independent and nonbiased, opinion of hotels, restaurants and B&Bs. Search for London Hotels and check recent feedback before confirming your booking. In particular, it's useful to review comments relating to cleanliness, helpfulness of staff and traffic noise (which are important factors but not easy to assess on standard websites). Trip Advisor provides a second sight when booking an unknown hotel, and allows the booker to book with confidence.

Visitbristol.co.uk/conferences

Planning a conference can be a daunting task, especially if that conference also requires catering to be arranged, bedrooms to be booked and entertainment programmes to be organised. Destination Bristol can help you with all aspects of your event. As well as running a free venue finding service for meeting and conference rooms, we can also find and negotiate bedroom bookings for groups and conference delegates, and provide travel and transport advice.

Visitlondon.com

A valuable source of information on 'all things London'. If your executive has an opportunity for some free time in London then this website will provide ideas catering for all tastes and interests. Take a virtual tour of London, download the official London app, and search for special offers for Theatre Tickets and Restaurant Deals and source essential traveller information.

World-airport-codes.com

Search for the correct airport code for your destination airport. World Airport Codes is the place to find airport codes, abbreviations, runway lengths and other airport information for nearly every airport worldwide. World Airport Codes is useful when researching an unfamiliar airport destination.

Glossary

Glossary

1 to 1	1 to 1s or One to Ones or 121s: are individual meetings between an employee and their line manager. They are confidential, two-way and held away from the remainder of the team, often by conference call or face to face. Content will include general updates, review and prioritisation of tasks. 1 to 1s provide an opportunity to talk through key issues and agree strategy.
AV – Audio Visual	Using sight and sound together e.g. a Video Conference.
Android	Android is a smartphone operating system (OS) developed by Google.
App	App is short for 'application' which is the same thing as a software program. While an app may refer to a program for any hardware platform, it is most often used to describe programs for mobile devices, such as smartphones and tablets.
Availability	The times and dates available to attend a meeting.
Board Member	A member of the Board of Directors.
Boutique Hotel	Boutique hotel is a term used in North America and the United Kingdom to describe an intimate, usually luxurious or quirky hotel. Boutique hotel rates are often sold at premium prices.
Brasserie	An informal restaurant, especially one in France or modelled on a French restaurant and with a large selection of drinks.
Bridge Number	The shared telephone number given to attendees of a conference call. The number which connects the callers.
Business Executive	A key employee who has major managerial and administrative authority within a company. Executives are the most senior level of employees in the business.
CEO	Chief Executive Officer, who may also be the Chairman of the Board or President.
CFO	Chief Financial Officer, who may also be known as the Executive Vice President
City of London	The business and financial Centre of London, also informally referred to as The Square Mile.

Cloud	The practice of using a network of remote servers hosted on the Internet to store, manage, and process data, rather than a local server.
Company Headquarters	Company or Corporate headquarters is the part of a company structure that deals with important tasks such as strategic planning, corporate communications, taxes, law, marketing, finance, human resources, and information technology. Company headquarters takes responsibility for the overall success of the business, and ensures Corporate Governance.
Company Secretary	Responsible for the efficient administration of a company, particularly with regard to ensuring compliance with statutory and regulatory requirements.
Concierge	In hotels, a concierge assists guests with various tasks such as making restaurant reservations, arranging for spa services, booking transportation (private drivers, airplanes, taxis, etc.), procurement of tickets to special events and assisting with various additional travel arrangements and tours of local attractions. A useful source of local information.
Conference Call	A meeting where participants join via a phone call (not a face to face), often using a conference bridge.
Configuration	The way a software program or device is set up for a particular computer, computer system, or task. The way in which email settings are configured or the diary is configured to a particular specification.
Corporate	Relating to a corporation, a large company or group.
Diary Management	Management of an executive's office diary, usually by a Personal or Executive Assistant.
Delegate	1. A person authorized to act as representative for another; a deputy or agent. 2. A representative at a conference or convention. 3. A PA awarded delegate permissions on Outlook (to manage the diary on another's behalf).
Device	An item of IT hardware which is mobile e.g. tablet, notebook, smartphone or laptop.
Diary Protocol	Establishing the responsibilities and process of diary management, between an executive and their PA.

Domestic Flight	A flight where the departure and the arrival take place in the same country.
Dow Jones	The US stock market
Downwards vertical	Anything and anyone below your executive's position.
Entrepreneur	A person who sets up a business or businesses, taking on financial risks in the hope of profit.
Executive	A senior manager in a corporation.
FTE	A full time employee of a company.
FTSE 100	Is a share index of the 100 most highly capitalised UK companies listed on the London Stock Exchange.
Face to Face	A meeting where attendees attend in person.
Facilitator	A facilitator helps a group of people in a business to reach an outcome or decision, for which everyone will take responsibility and be fully committed. A facilitator helps by providing a structure to a process. A facilitator doesn't lead, but rather guides.
Gatekeeper	A person who controls access to something or someone. A PA who screens calls and holds the diary of an executive is also known as the gatekeeper.
Headhunting	When a recruiter or employer, identifies and approaches, a suitable person already employed elsewhere, to fill a job vacancy.
HNWI	A high net worth individual. An individual with liquid assets in excess of £1M.
Inbound Flight	Inbound is the return sector of the flight, the flight which is arriving at your starting point of travel.
Incumbent	The current holder of a particular job or office.
Industry	Any general business activity or commercial enterprise that can be categorised from others, such as the legal industry or the finance industry.
Interstate	Existing or carried on between states, especially of the US (interstate travel is travel between states).
Kaizen	Japanese term for a gradual approach to ever higher standards in quality enhancement and waste reduction, through small but continual improvements, involving everyone from the CEO to the lowest level workers.
Late Availability	When hotels upload their unsold rooms, at hugely discounted prices on booking websites, the room rates are referred to as Late Availability rates.

Layover	Period of time spent by a passenger at an airport waiting for a connecting flight.
Leadership Group	The most senior executives in the business.
Long Haul	Flights over 6 hours in duration.
Loyalty Card	In the UK a loyalty card (US a discount card, club card or rewards card) will allow the user to collect points, and obtain discounts against future purchases.
Mentee	A person who is advised, trained, or counselled by a mentor.
Mentor	A mentor in the workplace is a person who provides guidance to a less-experienced employee, the mentee. A mentor may be another employee of the company, or may be an external professional. The mentor is a role model who shares knowledge and advice to help the employee grow professionally. Mentoring relationships benefit the employee, as well as the employer and mentor, and have long-term advantage
MS Exchange	A popular e-mail messaging system from Microsoft that runs on Windows servers. The server side is Microsoft Exchange Server and the featured client program is Microsoft Outlook, which includes contacts and calendaring.
Non-executive Director	A non-executive director (abbreviated to non-exec, NED or NXD) or outside director, is a member of the board of directors of a company, or organisation, who does not form part of the executive management team.
Organizational Culture	The values and behaviours that contribute to the unique social and psychological environment of an organization. Organizational culture includes an organization's expectations, experiences, philosophy, and values that hold it together, and is expressed in its self-image, inner workings, interactions with the outside world, and future expectations. It is based on shared attitudes, beliefs, customs, and written and unwritten rules that have been developed over time and are considered valid. Also called corporate culture, it's shown in (1) the ways the organization conducts its business, treats its employees,

customers, and the wider community, (2) the extent to which freedom is allowed in decision making, developing new ideas, and personal .

Outbound Flight	Outbound is the departing flight, the flight which is leaving your starting point of travel.
Plenary	A session of a conference or other meeting at which all members are expected to attend.
Postcode	UK equivalent of ZIP code: a code of letters and digits added to a postal address to aid in the sorting of mail.
Power Bank	Power banks serve as an 'extra battery' or external charger for your phone or other electronic devices.
Predecessor	A person who held a job or office before the current holder.
Preferred Supplier	Supplier or Vendor that has a continuing arrangement to provide a business or organisation with products or services, often at a reduced price.
President	In the US, the Chairman of the Board of Directors may be called the President.
Procurement	The act of obtaining or buying goods and services.
Private Dining	A private room reserved for a private party of diners. Private Dining provides discreet and uninterrupted service in a confidential environment, often used for business dinners and client entertainment.
Re-occurring Meeting	When a particular meeting and topic is scheduled on a repeat basis e.g. weekly, fortnightly or monthly, using the re-occurring tool in Outlook.
Road Warrior	A business traveller who flies in excess of 40 flights per annum.
Sector	A part or division of a national economy e.g. public, private, not for profit
Service Charge	A service fee, service charge, or surcharge is a fee added to a customer's bill, usually as a percentage of the total amount payable. Restaurants charging service charges in lieu of tips must distribute them to their wait staff in some US states. In the UK this is not always the case and some suppliers keep the tips, and do not share with the employees.
Serviced Apartment	Rentable accommodation consisting of studios and 1-3 bed apartments. Commonly considered for long-term letting solutions as a cheaper alternative to hotel daily room rates. Apartments are 'serviced' by

	a cleaner, laundry services are available and food boxes can be ordered prior to arrival.
Showaround	A representative of a hotel provides a viewing of bedrooms, conference facilities and restaurant available for hire to prospective clients.
Smartphone	A smartphone is a mobile phone that includes advanced functionality beyond making phone calls and sending text messages. Most smartphones have the capability to display photos, play videos, check and send e-mail, and surf the Web.
Soft Skills	Your personal attributes, your emotional intelligence.
Specialism	A field of specialization within an industry e.g. Legal PA, Medical PA, Finance PA.
Square Mile	The informal name for 'The City of London' an area which covers around 1.1 square miles. Bordered by the River Thames to the south, Barbican to the north, Aldgate in the east and Chancery Lane to the west.
SWOT Analysis	Situation analysis in which internal strengths and weaknesses of an organization, and external opportunities and threats faced by it are closely examined to chart a strategy. SWOT stands for strengths, weaknesses, opportunities, and threats.
Studio Apartment	A small apartment which combines living room, bedroom, and kitchenette into a single room.
Summit	A meeting of the highest level of officials, especially the diplomatic level of heads of government or a conference of highest-level officials or managers in a business.
Super Skill	The skills associated with being a successful PA.
Sync	To synchronise multiple devices, to ensure that data is replicated and accessible across all devices.
Tablet Computer	A tablet, or tablet PC, is a portable computer that is operated via a touch screen. Most tablets are slightly smaller and weigh less than the average laptop. While some tablets include fold out keyboards, others only offer touch screen input.
Tip	A tip or gratuity is a voluntary additional payment made for services received at a restaurant or hotel.
Town Hall	A town hall meeting is an informal public meeting, function, or event derived from the traditional town meetings of New England. Often involving all levels

	of employees to communicate company news or announcements.
Transit	When a person is at the point of travelling from one destination to another.
Tray Charge	An additional fixed charge added for room service delivery in City hotels.
Tube	London's underground rail system – informally called 'The Tube' by Londoners.
Upwards Vertical	Anything and anyone above your executive's position.
Virtual Meeting	Is an event or series of events where participants join in from multiple locations remotely. A virtual meeting may be held in "real time" where everyone is participating at the same time, often by teleconference or video conference.
Webcast	A webcast is a media presentation distributed over the Internet using streaming media. Webcasting is also used extensively in the commercial sector for investor relations presentations (such as annual general meetings).
Webinar	A Web based seminar.
Wi-Fi	Technology that allows an electronic device to exchange data wirelessly.
In-room Wi-Fi	Wi-Fi which is available inside the hotel bedroom as opposed to public areas.
Workshop	An educational seminar or series of meetings emphasizing interaction and exchange of information among a usually small number of participants
WPM	Words per minute (typing speed count).

Thank you for purchasing my book. I hope you've found 'How to be a PA' useful, practical and empowering. I've thoroughly enjoyed writing it, and sharing my experience with you. Please connect with me on LinkedIn, follow @howtobeapa on Twitter, tell your peers about this book, and please leave a review on Amazon. I wish you every success throughout your enjoyable and rewarding career - as a PA.

Maria Fuller, Author and EA.
UK, June 2016.

8129409R00153

Printed in Germany
by Amazon Distribution
GmbH, Leipzig